LONDON'S INDUSTRIAL PAST

MARK AMIES

AMBERLEY

(Trumans Beer Company)

Front cover: Workers leaving the Airco factory, Colindale, 1917. (London Borough of Barnet)
Rear cover: Beecham's factory, Brentford, in the 1970s. (GlaxoSmithKline)

First published 2020

Amberley Publishing
The Hill, Stroud,
Gloucestershire, GL5 4EP

www.amberley-books.com

ISBN: 978 1 4456 9802 1 (print)
ISBN: 978 1 4456 9803 8 (ebook)

British Library Cataloguing in Publication Data.
A catalogue record for this book is available from the British Library.

Typeset in 10pt on 14pt Celeste.
Origination by Amberley Publishing.
Printed in the UK.

Contents

Foreword

Mark is an urban archaeologist. Where others might seek the relics and remains of ancient cultures and civilisations buried deep, shards and fragments of lost worlds, so Mr Amies is constantly scouring the city for the physical heritage and the still vivid memories of our recent industrial past. A world not so much lost as misplaced, hiding in plain sight, among the constantly changing cityscape.

He loves a factory. Where many might dismiss the brute architecture of old manufacturing, Mark sees it as a repository of so many of our collective stories. Our tales and those of our parents and grandparents, who worked those machines, manned those lines, drove those engines, lived their lives on the factory floor. Their stories are there in the bricks and ironwork, the vast yards and canteens, the storerooms and warehouses, the forgotten factory expanses of Cricklewood and Croydon, Park Royal, Bermondsey and Battersea, which once gave employment to so many.

Not so long ago London was a dirty, sooty city, the Thames as the centre of a teeming metropolis, which made stuff; big stuff; noisy, important, tasty, smelly, powerful things to drive our economy and drive up the Great West Road. From cars to chocolates, munitions to musical instruments, flying machines to malt vinegar. They were all made in the capital.

We have lost so many of those magnificent monuments to the machine age, but seek and you shall find. Read and you shall discover a time when London was once the industrial powerhouse of the world.

Robert Elms
October 2019

Introduction

Back in December 2018 I started a series of twenty-minute slots on BBC Radio London's *Robert Elms Show*. The content of these broadcasts was the inspiration for this book, and I am indebted to Robert and his team for their support and enthusiasm. I have covered many different aspects of London's manufacturing past, with a focus on the twentieth century, as I felt this was something that the listeners could relate to.

My desire with this publication is to show to the reader what was, and in many cases, is no more. Industry is more than just product and profit: it's about people, and their daily efforts to make things of all kinds. From the mundane to the sophisticated, and from the frivolous to the essential, London and its workers have made all manner of everyday products. However, the days of large factories with saw-tooth roofs and smoking chimneys have long passed, and in our digital age, it is the steel and glass office building where so many of the capital city's workers go. Large numbers of the factory buildings have been swept away and replaced by apartment blocks or corrugated steel-clad retail and storage sheds, for goods made in other countries.

Not all is lost, though. We do have plenty of these impressive structures left, to remind us of what London once made. Those that do stand have been repurposed into different kinds of commerce or turned into accommodation, and it is just as well they have or they too may have gone. One only has to go back to the bank holiday weekend of September 1980, when the once imperious-looking Firestone Tyre & Rubber building was ruthlessly demolished by desperate developers. That incident stirred a group of like-minded individuals to start pressure groups, such as the Twentieth Century Society, to focus the public's mind on preserving these symbols of London's manufactories. We can thank these caring people for the saving of other buildings, like the art deco classic Hoover Building on the A40 Western Avenue in Perivale.

Having spent so many broadcasts talking about London's industrial past, and relying on 'word pictures', this book was at last an opportunity to show people what was once a physical presence in the landscape. When I set out on the planning of the content, I had high hopes (as one does); however, obtaining archive images is not an easy, quick or cheap task. So with that in mind, I have to state quite clearly that the book does not show everything I wanted. However, what I have managed to claw in will hopefully provide the reader with a decent enough visual feast.

I hope that you enjoy the following pages, and that they may (if you are of the enquiring type) lead you to do your own research. One thing I must say is that it is important to share what you find with others. I stress this because London's industrial past is something that everyone can be interested in, because its very essence was people, and people of all types, from the person who cleaned the spaces in the buildings to the people who presided over them. London's industrial past is London's past, and they are inextricably entwined.

Mark Amies
September 2019

Acknowledgements & Image Credits

I would like to thank the following for their assistance and support:

My wife for her support and encouragement.
My parents, for initiating my interest in the subject from a young age, and for their financial assistance with image costs.
Robert Elms and his producer at BBC Radio London, Sarah Bateson, for their support over the first year of my broadcasting efforts.
Mr Hugh Petrie at London Borough of Barnet Local History Studies Archive.
Mr James Marshall at London Borough of Hounslow Archives for his encouragement and assistance.
Jill Moretto, the company archivist at GlaxoSmithkline.
The Ford Motor Company.
Pladis UK.
My workplace at the Warburg Institute for their support.
Josh at Modernism in Metroland and Paul Talling of Derelict London for showing me that I could do this.
Mr Lukas Novotny for letting me use his supremely good illustrations.
The Handley Page Association.
John Simpson at Dubreq.
Gary and Frank at The Peek Frean Museum, Bermondsey.
The Brighton Toy Museum.

Unless stated, all images are by the author.

Brewing

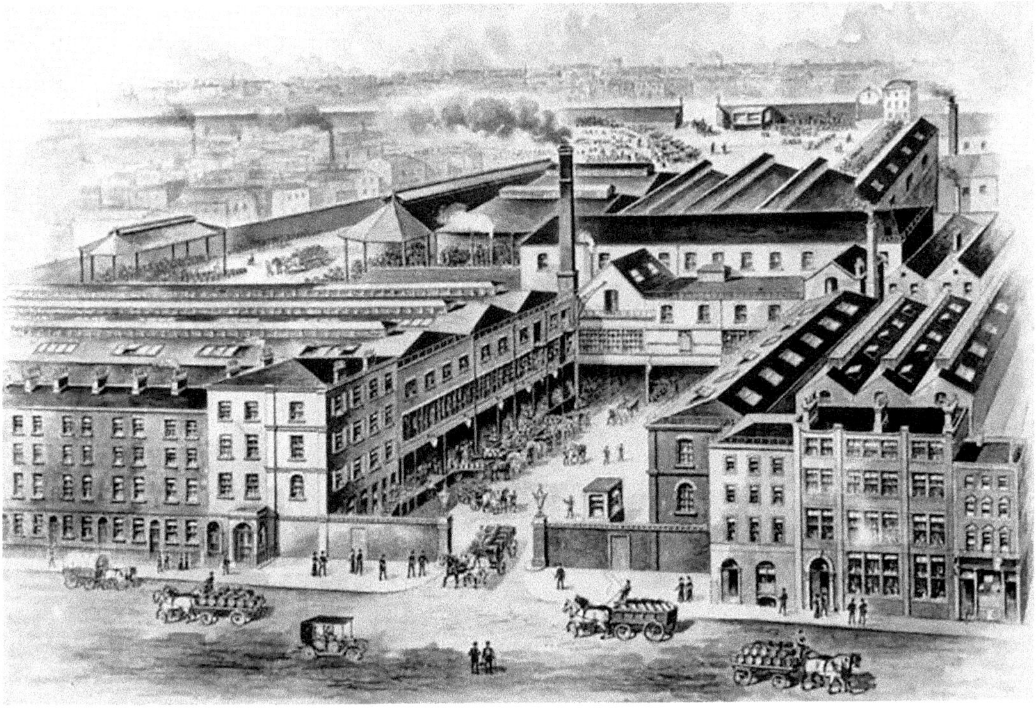

The Whitbread brewery, Chiswell Street, *c.* 1900. (Brewery History Society)

Courage, Bermondsey

The Anchor Brewhouse, on the south side of Tower Bridge, is a well-known landmark that was redeveloped as apartments, shops and restaurants in the late 1980s. In 1787 John Courage took over the existing brewery on this site and developed his business. The site was vast, occupying a number of blocks nearby for all associated elements of production, and included a pub called the Anchor Tap, which survives (see image left). The brewery closed in 1982. Courage beers are now brewed in the Midlands by the brand's owner, Marston's. (Johnny Homer)

Trumans, Whitechapel
The Black Eagle Brewery in Brick Lane was established in 1666 and Joseph Truman took it over in 1694. His descendant Ben Truman became involved in 1722 and really developed the business. He was knighted in 1760 and became one of the first brewery barons. After his death in 1780, the Hanbury and Buxton families joined the company. The brewery grew and grew, becoming a local landmark with its prominent brick chimney. The complex was like a small town, covering ten acres. It had its own cooperage, wheelwrights, farriers, carpenters, paint shop and artists' studio. Trumans was taken over by Grand Metropolitan in 1971 and the Black Eagle Brewery closed in 1989. The Truman name returned in 2010, and brews in Hackney Wick. (Trumans Beer Company)

Watneys, Pimlico and Mortlake

Starting off in the Stag brewery in Pimlico (above) in 1837, Watney's merged with Coombe & Reid in 1898. The famous Red Barrel beer was launched in 1930. By 1959 the company had moved out of Pimlico and the site was extensively redeveloped as an office development called Stag Place. The pre-existing Phillips brewery in Mortlake (left) became the company's new home. Watney Mann (as it became) was bought by Grand Metropolitan in 1972 and merged with Trumans. By the late 1980s the Watney's brand was phased out. The Mortlake site ended its days owned by the giant ABInBev, producing Budweiser and Michleob beers. Production ceased in 2010 and the site has now been redeveloped as apartments. (Brewery History Society)

Whitbread, City of London

Whitbread was established at 52 Chiswell Street, not far from the modern Barbican development, in 1749 by Samuel Whitbread. By 1780 it claimed to be the world's largest brewery. In 1785 Whitbread was one of the first brewers to use a steam engine, using it for grinding malt and raising the liquor. Although the main production from the start was porter, by 1834 the company moved on to pale ale, which had become more popular. Despite being one of London's biggest producers, Whitbread stopped brewing at Chiswell Street in 1976, having built a huge new super-brewery in Luton in preparation. The original brewery is now a conference and event facility, simply called 'The Brewery'. Whitbread pulled out of the drinks business in 2001 and its main business is now hotels and restaurants.

Young's, Wandsworth
The Ram Brewery, on Ram Street, dates from 1675 and was acquired by Charles Young in 1831. Young & Co. was a highly successful and much-loved brewer, and Young's Best Bitter was considered by many to be one of London's great beers. To the great disappointment of its fans, the company closed the brewery in 2006, after it merged with Charles Wells of Bedford. The chairman, Charles Young, died literally days before the closure. The brewery was redeveloped as 'Ram Quarter' but brewing still continues there in the form of a 'nano-brewery', to continue a sense of tradition and to maintain the site as Britain's oldest continually operated brewery. (Paul Talling/derelictLondon.com)

Guinness, Park Royal

Until the emergence of craft and micro-breweries in the early 2000s, the Guinness facility had been the most recent of the capital's breweries. Designed by Sir Giles Gilbert Scott and built between 1933 and 1936, this huge complex of buildings stood beside the Great Western Railway on what had once been the former Agricultural Society showground. Three main structures dominated the site, the malthouse, the brewhouse and the storehouse, all connected by bridges, and there was a large open reservoir to feed the facility. At its height, in the 1950s, Guinness employed 1,500 workers, who were well looked after, with not only sports and social clubs, but also accommodation. Sadly, in 2005 the company decided to cease production at Park Royal, and shortly afterwards the site was cleared. The parent company, Diageo, has an office complex on the site and the rest is given over to residential blocks. (Upper: Guinness Archive/Diageo Ireland)

Toys

Lesney Matchbox 1957 catalogue cover. (Brighton Toy Museum)

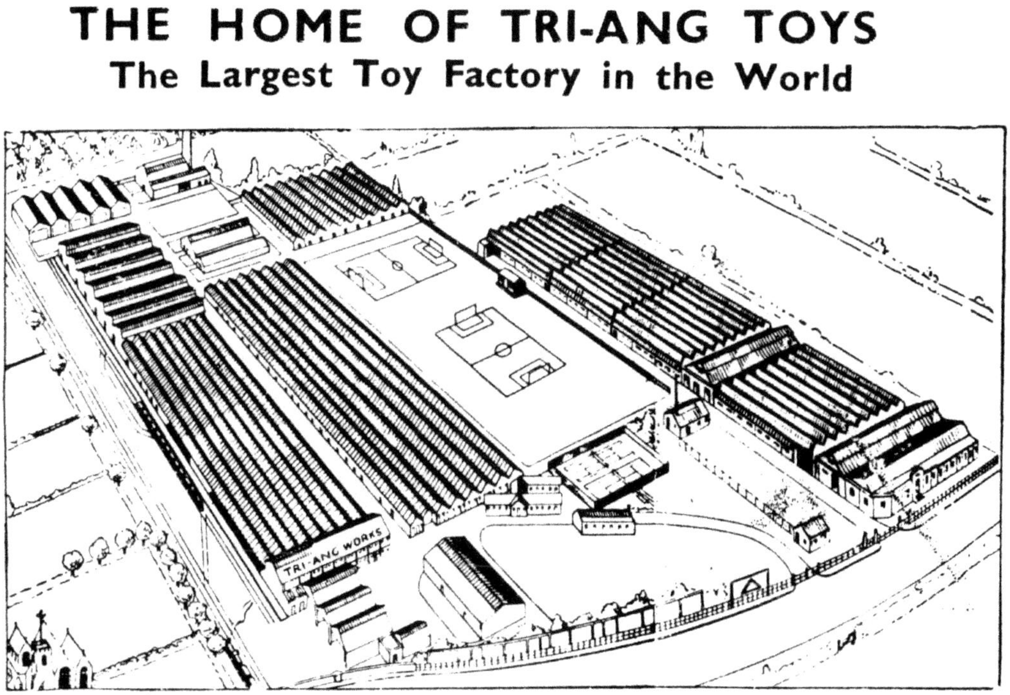

Tri-ang, Merton

The three Lines brothers formed their toy company in 1919 on the Old Kent Road, south-east London, using the brand name 'Triangtois'. Sales were so good that by 1923 the company was able to move to a 27-acre site in Merton, conveniently sited next to the main railway line. The company was happy to boast that this was 'The Largest Toy Factory in the World'. A huge selection of toys were made, from bicycles to prams, tinplate vehicles and dolls. A measure of the plant's productivity is that it had increased its workforce from 500 at the time of opening to 2,000 by 1932. (Upper: Brighton Toy Museum, Lower: Graces Guide)

Like many manufacturers in the Second World War, Lines Brothers turned over to the making of weapons, and its main output was the Sten submachine gun. Walter Lines, a gifted designer, actually improved the design of the Sten, making it lighter and more efficient. By the end of the war, the Merton plant had turned out a million of the guns. One of the many toy lines produced was the range of clockwork 'Minic' vehicles, made from the 1930s to the 1950s. Despite continued expansion, and taking over other toy-makers, by 1971 debts and the failure of overseas markets saw the Lines Brothers business being broken up, and the Merton factory closed in 1972. The site is now a large trading estate. (Upper: Brett Smuda, Lower: Graces Guide)

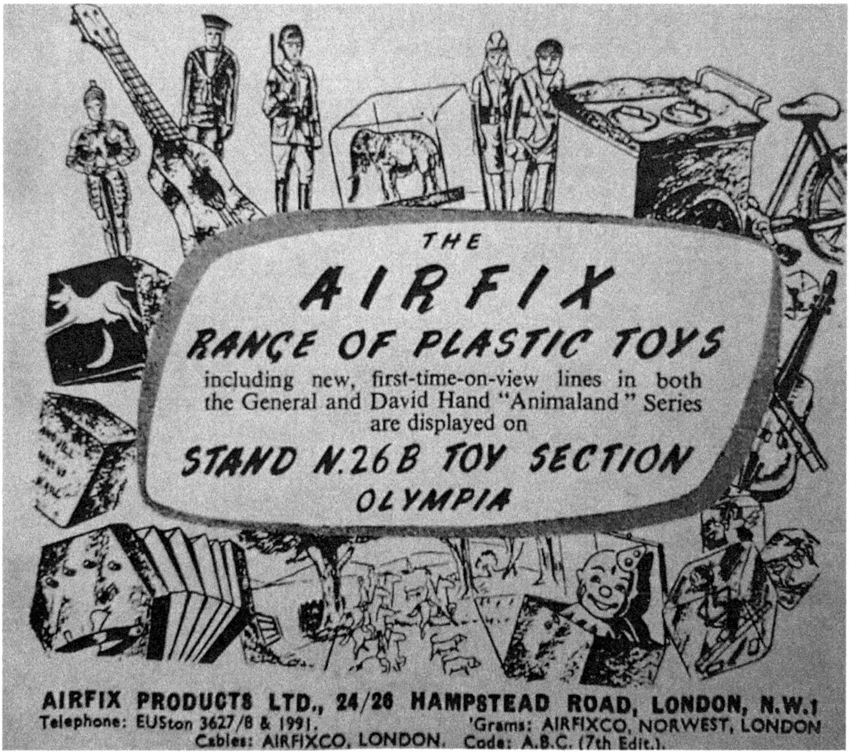

Airfix, Wandsworth

The iconic plastic construction kit maker was founded in 1939 by Hungarian emigre Nicholas Kove, who started making air-filled plastic toys (which is how the name was derived). The company's early premises were near Euston, but then it moved out to a larger factory off Garratt Lane, Earlsfield, which had originally been the Columbia gramophone factory. A change of ownership in the early 1980s saw production cease, and the site is now called the Riverside Business Centre. Airfix carries on to this day, as part of the Hornby group. (Upper: Graces Guide, Lower: Arthur Ward)

DESCRIPTIVE PRICE LIST

OF

W. BRITAIN & SONS'

CELEBRATED

Automatic and Scientific

CLOCKWORK MODELS, TOYS, &c.

28, LAMBTON ROAD,

HORNSEY RISE, LONDON, N.

Britains, Walthamstow

The company was started in 1893 in a house on Lambton Road, Hornsey, by William Britain, who had invented the hollow casting of lead toy soldiers. As time went on increased production saw the purchasing of an adjoining property, and then rebuilding. Britains produced a bewildering range of military models, and after the First World War they developed a range of farm models, perhaps realising the need to broaden their appeal to girls in a more peaceful period. In 1931 the company opened a factory in Stirling Road, Walthamstow. By 1949 another factory opened in Sutherland Road, and then in the late 1960s there was a move again to a new site in Blackhorse Road. Incredibly surviving under family ownership for nearly a century, the company was taken over in 1984 and the factory closed in 1991.
(Graces Guide)

Lesney, Hackney

Leslie and Rodney Smith (who were not related) started a small die-casting company in 1947, and they used their Christian names to create the name, Lesney. The first workshop was in an old pub called the Rifleman, in Edmonton. Originally undertaking industrial contracts, they realised they needed to keep busy in slack periods. Their chief engineer, Jack Odell, had created a small model road roller that his daughter could fit in a matchbox to take to school, and this was the idea that started what would become a huge business. (Author's Collection)

The company went from strength to strength, and by 1965 it had built a huge new plant in Homerton, next to the Lee Navigation waterway. Large numbers of local people were employed, many being brought in by the company's own fleet of old double-decker buses. Lesney products were awarded two Queen's Export awards in the late 1960s. Sadly, the following decade proved harder for them and by 1982 Lesney went bankrupt. Under new ownership the factories stayed open until the late 1980s. Production moved to South East Asia, and the Matchbox brand is currently owned by Mattel. The image below shows the plant in December 1981. (Upper: London Borough of Hackney, Lower: Neil Martinson)

Aircraft

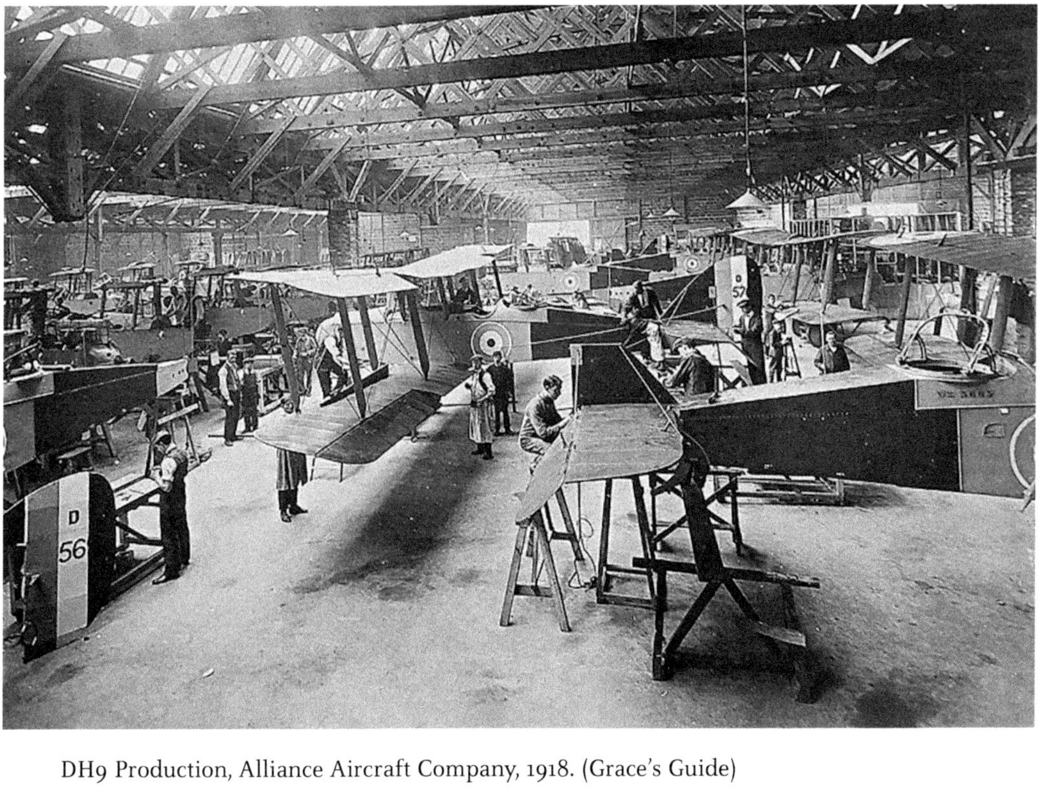

DH9 Production, Alliance Aircraft Company, 1918. (Grace's Guide)

RED HILL, HYDE, HENDON.

Airco, Colindale

Otherwise known as the Aircraft Manufacturing Company Limited, Airco was founded in 1912 by George Holt Thomas. A factory complex was built on both sides of the Hyde (a section of the A5 Edgware Road) at Colindale, to meet the increasing demand for military aircraft. In the image above it is possible to see the area before the company arrived, and the lower image was taken shortly after the First World War by the company's aerial photography division. Holt Thomas proudly claimed it was the world's largest aircraft factory and it is easy to see why. The location was picked because of the proximity to Hendon Aerodrome. In 1917 a branch line was run off the London & North Western Railway line near Aerodrome Road, and ran the perimeter of the aerodrome, right up to the factory, with a level crossing, so materials and parts could be supplied directly. (London Borough of Barnet)

The factory employed up to 8,000 people, of both sexes, and at the peak of production it turned out a complete aircraft every forty-five minutes. Many different skills and trades were employed, from wood and metalworking to fabric-cutting, stitching and doping (the coating of the fabric with treatment) and rigging. The chief designer was Geoffrey de Havilland, and all the company's aircraft carried his initials, 'DH', and ran as a series from DH1 to DH18. The image above shows workers leaving the factory on Annesley Road to catch trams, taking them as far as Acton. The image below shows the same building as it was in 2019, in use as a car tyre and exhaust replacement garage. It is one of just three original buildings that survive, the others being the offices and an electricity sub-station. (Upper: London Borough of Barnet)

The image above shows workers in winter 1917, walking past some of the other assembly sheds. These buildings were swept away in the 1980s, to be replaced by a small retail park, seen in the image below. On the other side of the road stood the largest factory space, known as 'Block G', which had an umbrella-type roof, allowing for a vast space unsupported by columns, ideal for production. The end of the war saw Airco struggle to survive, moving into aerial photography and motor repairs, and by 1920 the company was sold to BSA. Within a few years the site had been sold off to various manufacturers, specifically General Motors and Phoenix Telephone. The area is now dominated by retailers and housing, with one marker to the past being a residential road named Airco Close, erected in the early 2000s. (Upper: London Borough of Barnet)

The Main Entrance to the Works of the Grahame-White Company.

Grahame-White, Colindale

Claude Grahame-White was one of the UK's aviation pioneers and established the London Aerodrome at Hendon in 1910. The aerodrome became a magnet for early aviators and Grahame-White believed that Hendon could become London's first 'Airport'. The war stopped that but he put his efforts into aircraft-making, both under licence and his own designs. The Air Ministry took over Hendon during the First World War and never gave it back – apparently due to unresolved debts. Grahame White's Watch Office, which faced the airfield and was joined by a spine to the main entrance building, has been recreated at the RAF Museum nearby. (London Borough of Barnet)

Handley Page, Cricklewood

Frederick Handley Page was one of Britain's great aviation figures, and started manufacturing his aircraft in Barking in 1909. By 1912 he had moved to Cricklewood, and occupied a large building where the Matalan clothes store is currently. Handley Page specialised in heavy bombers, and his first one, the o/100 (similar to the image above), was moved by road to Hendon Aerodrome in December 1915. Within a short time the company had moved to much larger premises on the other side of the railway, affording it room for its own airfield. (Upper: Graces Guide, Lower: Handley Page Association)

In the image above, taken from a Handley Page aircraft, you can see the works and airfield just off Claremont Road, with the railway sidings to the left. Such was the demand for aircraft in the war that the company subcontracted work out to Harris Lebus, the furniture makers in Tottenham. By 1929, suburban and industrial growth in the area made the airfield impractical, and Handley Page opened a new factory and airfield further out in Radlett, Hertfordshire. However, the Cricklewood site was kept for production right up until 1964. The company was dissolved in 1969 and the factory site is now a trading estate. (Handley Page Association)

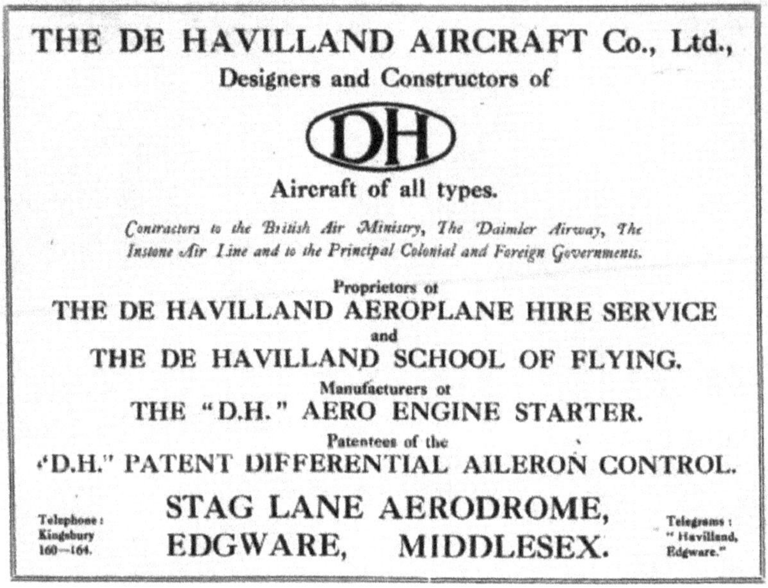

THE DE HAVILLAND AIRCRAFT Co., Ltd.,
Designers and Constructors of
DH
Aircraft of all types.
Contractors to the British Air Ministry, The Daimler Airway, The Instone Air Line and to the Principal Colonial and Foreign Governments.
Proprietors of
THE DE HAVILLAND AEROPLANE HIRE SERVICE
and
THE DE HAVILLAND SCHOOL OF FLYING.
Manufacturers of
THE "D.H." AERO ENGINE STARTER.
Patentees of the
"D.H." PATENT DIFFERENTIAL AILERON CONTROL.
Telephone: Kingsbury 160–164.
STAG LANE AERODROME, EDGWARE, MIDDLESEX.
Telegrams: "Havilland, Edgware."

De Havilland, Kingsbury

In 1915 the London & Provincial Aviation Company opened an aerodrome near Stag Lane in Kingsbury as a training base. By 1922 the ex-Airco designer Geoffrey de Havilland had purchased the site and started making his own aircraft, which were aimed at the civilian leisure market. The company's highly successful 'Moth' series of aeroplanes were flown by well-heeled enthusiasts, and among the customers were the famous aviator Amy Johnson and her husband Jim Mollison. As you can see in the lower image, encroaching suburban settlement was making flying more of a problem, and by 1934 it was time for de Havilland to find a new site for its aircraft manufacturing. The company moved out to Hatfield in Hertfordshire. The Kingsbury airfield was sold off to developers for what became the new suburb of Queensbury. (Upper: Graces Guide, Lower: BAE Systems)

The image above shows the old factory hangar buildings after the new roads were put in. One of them, named after Jim Mollison (Mollison Way), follows the path of the old runway. De Havilland retained Stag Lane to manufacture engines and propellers. The main office building is shown in the 1950s below. In 1960 De Havilland became part of the Hawker Siddeley group. The site was used by Banks Automated Clearing Services (BACS) from 1968 for its computers, joined by what became British Telecom in 1976, which used other buildings as a temporary home for the International Telephone Exchange. The site is now housing. (Upper: BAE Systems, Lower: John Clemens/DH Aeronautical Tech Association)

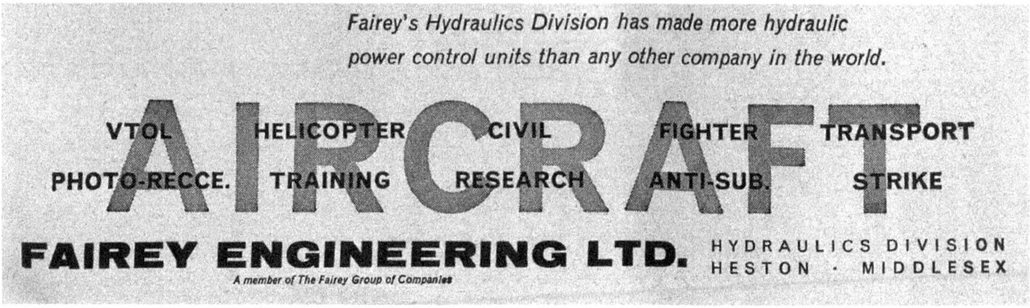

Fairey Aviation, Hayes and Heston
Richard Fairey brought his aviation company to Hayes in 1915. The company had a reputation for innovative design. Its best-known aircraft was the Fairey Swordfish, used very effectively by the Fleet Air Arm in the Second World War to launch torpedoes. After the war, Fairey explored the boundaries of delta-shaped wings for high speed flying research. This resulted in the beautiful Fairey Delta Two, which is illustrated by the Topps gum card below. In 1960, under Government pressure to rationalise the aviation industry, Fairey was merged with Westland. Aircraft production stopped at this point and work continued in specialist military equipment at the Hayes and Heston sites. The remaining buildings were vacated in the 1990s, and the remnants of the company exist as Spectris PLC. (Author's Collection)

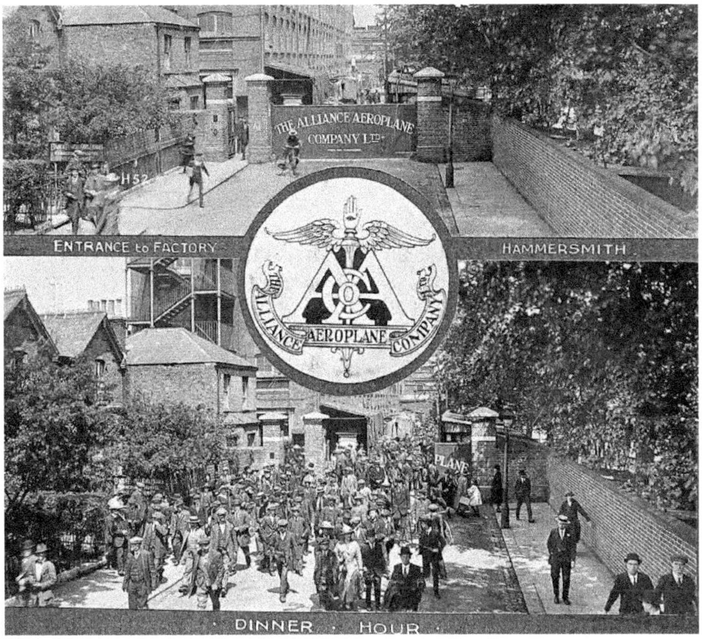

Alliance, Hammersmith and Acton

Founded by the furniture makers Waring & Gillow and the Nieuport aircraft company in 1918 to meet warplane demand, production was at Waring's factory in Hammersmith. The company used its skills in woodworking and acquired new ones like rigging and metalworking. An airfield was needed, so the existing Acton Aerodrome was taken over. Semi-finished aeroplanes were brought out from Hammersmith to Acton by road, and assembled in the huge hangers that lined one side of the airfield. Like many other military aircraft-makers after the war, Alliance was unable to continue and closed in 1920. (Graces Guide)

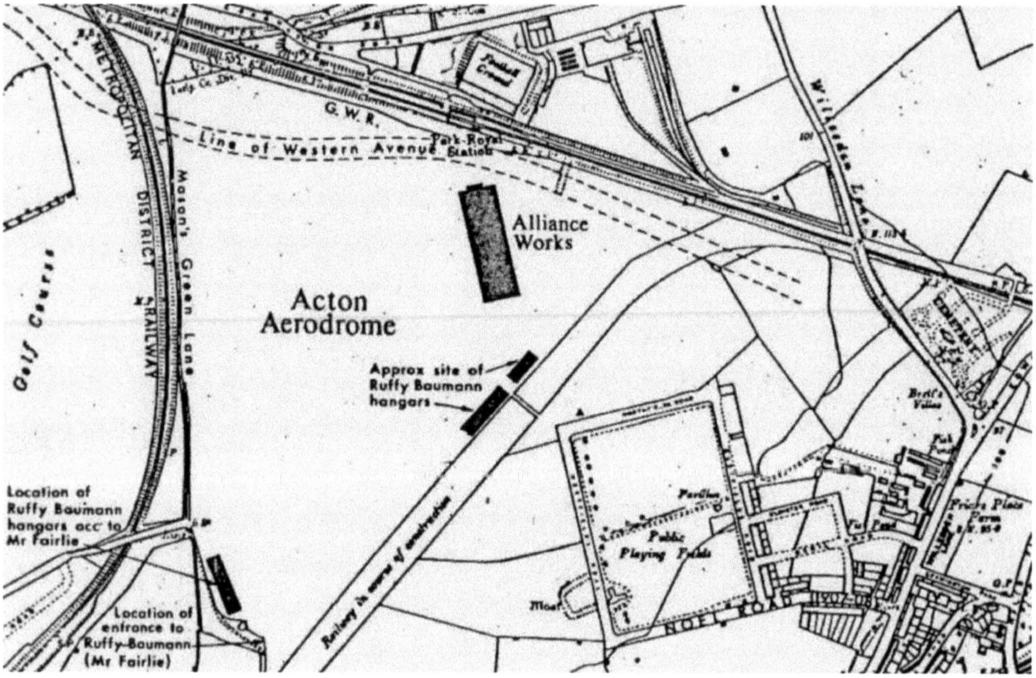

The factory buildings at Acton were taken over by other manufacturers, most notably the French car maker Renault. The company's name lives on in the form of Alliance Road, which passes the front of the hangars. In the image below you can see one of the remaining buildings, including the steelwork that held up the roof. This particular building is currently used by a film and television production company. The rest of the airfield was built over in the 1930s for industrial purposes, becoming another section of the Park Royal industrial estate. (Upper: Author's Collection)

Cars

Chevrolet van assembly, Colindale, *c.* 1928. (GM)

Ford, Dagenham
The first Ford factory outside North America was established in Trafford Park, Manchester, in 1911. The company realised it needed to be nearer the London market, but also nearer the European continent, so a site was found on the marshes at Dagenham in the late 1920s, Ford paying £167,000 for land. The task of cutting the first turf was given to Edsel Ford, son of the founder, Henry. To provide a firm footing for the new buildings, 22,000 concrete piles were driven down to the clay subsurface. By 1931 the first vehicles were rolling off the line. The site was self-sufficient in electricity, with its own on-site power station. The huge 'Ford' sign (seen in the 1960s image above), adorning the river side of the factory, was the largest neon-lit sign in Europe. The image below shows the site in the late 1930s. (Ford of Britain)

Over the years the Dagenham factory has given employment to thousands of people, producing many different vehicles that were amongst the best-selling and most popular cars of their time, including the Cortina (seen in the image below in 1963). The 1970s saw an era of strikes and Dagenham's status was affected. Vehicle production was gradually wound down, and the last car to be produced was the Ford Fiesta in 2002. Despite this loss, Ford continues to invest in the site and it now produces engines that go into the vehicles produced in Europe. (Ford of Britain)

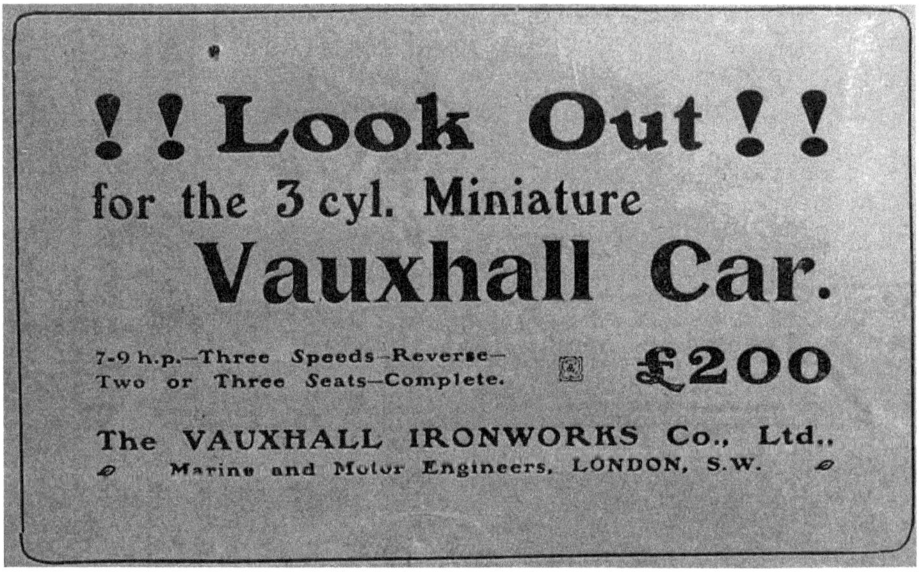

Vauxhall, Vauxhall
Starting as the Vauxhall Iron Works in 1857, the company made marine steam engines, and then moved onto internal combustion engines. Realising the potential for their use in motor cars, Vauxhall made its first vehicle in 1903, an example of which can be seen below. The original works was built on the site of a manor house called Falkes Hall, the home of a Plantagenet knight, and the company took his coat of arms, with the griffin as its badge. In 1905 the company moved to Luton, which happened to be the manor of Falkes de Breaute of Falkes Hall. In 1925 Vauxhall was bought by General Motors. In 2017, GM sold the Vauxhall brand to Peugeot PSA, and at the time of writing Peugeot is to merge with FiatChrysler. One hopes the Vauxhall name will survive. (Upper: Graces Guide, Lower: Vauxhall Heritage)

Bentley Motors, Cricklewood

Walter Owen Bentley had been an aero engine designer at the Wolseley Motors company and had designed the radial engine that was fitted into the famous First World War Sopwith Camel fighter plane. He started making cars in some garages in Marylebone in 1919. With orders coming in, it was clear he needed more space. He refused to move to the Midlands, where his suppliers were based, instead opting for a green-field site on the corner of Oxgate Lane and the Edgware Road in 1920. Bentley only produced 'rolling chassis', as customers would have bodies put on by separate coach-building companies, in most cases by the nearby Vanden Plas company in Kingsbury. The company developed its successful racing cars at the site, eventually winning at Le Mans every year between 1927 and 1930. Sadly, the 1929 financial crisis affected sales and payments, and in 1930 Rolls-Royce bought the company, moving production to Crewe in 1931. (Bentley Motors)

Chevrolet, Colindale

The huge General Motors company took over the disused Airco factory at Colindale in 1922 and assembled 'knocked-down' kits of Chevrolet trucks and vans. The building suited vehicle manufacturing, due to its large open space, allowing continuous line manufacturing. With GM's acquisition of Vauxhall, vehicle production moved to Luton in 1930 and the truck business was rebranded as Bedford. The vast factory was then turned over to making General Motors 'Frigidaire' refrigeration and air-conditioning products. (Upper: London Borough of Barnet, Lower: GM)

Hudson Motors, Chiswick

The American Hudson Motors company set up in Acton Vale originally in the early 1920s, moving to a purpose-built factory near the junction of the Chiswick roundabout and the Great West Road in 1926. Just like other US motor manufacturers, Hudson found a way around import restrictions by shipping in partly assembled cars or 'knocked-down' kits and finished them on site. The initial part of the building was brick finished, and had an elegant showroom facing onto the Great West Road. A feature of the frontage also included the mounting of the latest car on a plinth. The car was fitted with dressed mannequins and illuminated at night. (Charles K. Bowers)

The factory was enlarged greatly during the 1930s, allowing further advertising hoardings to be seen on Gunnersbury Avenue (the start of the North Circular). By the 1950s, and following a merger with Nash-Kelvinator, the factory was turned over to the manufacture of washing machines and refrigerators (in a similar way to the General Motors works at Colindale). The site is now a large B&Q store, but the old brick wall and gateposts on the Great West Road survive. (Upper: Ian Moore, Lower: Gunnersbury Park Museum)

Renault, Acton

Having been based in West Brompton since the 1910s, Renault decided it needed more space for both servicing and assembly of cars. It chose some of the buildings vacated by the Alliance aircraft company in 1925. The company made a range of cars at Acton right through until the late 1950s. The image above shows the assembling of Renault 4CV cars at Acton in the 1950s. The company maintained a presence on site with its main car showrooms and servicing department, continuing through to the present day. (Upper: Renault, Right: Graces Guide)

Clement-Talbot, Kensington

The Franco-British company built a showpiece factory on Barlby Road, Ladbroke Grove, in 1903. The look of the building very much projected the class of customer they were hoping to attract. The interior, which included a showroom, was incredibly grand. Originally French-made parts were assembled but by 1906 the company had become semi-independent and started designing and building their own vehicles. The business went through a number of changes, merging with Darraq and then Sunbeam, and was eventually taken over by the Rootes Group in 1936. Car manufacturing stopped shortly after, and the factory became a repair works and offices. By the late 1960s Rootes had been bought by Chrysler. The building has been restored and renamed Ladbroke Hall and is, aptly, the home of Sunbeam Studios, a photographic business. (Upper: Author's Collection, Lower: Anita Amies)

Chrysler, Kew

Chrysler set up a factory in the early 1920s, near Mortlake Road, Kew. The image above shows the artist's impression completed for the company. Like other American vehicle makers, Chrysler produced cars from knocked-down kits. The site was advantageous because it was next to the River Thames so parts could come via barge from the London docks. The cars were given names associated with the Surrey area, such as the Chrysler Kew and Wimbledon. (Upper: FiatChrysler, Lower: London Bus Museum (Brooklands))

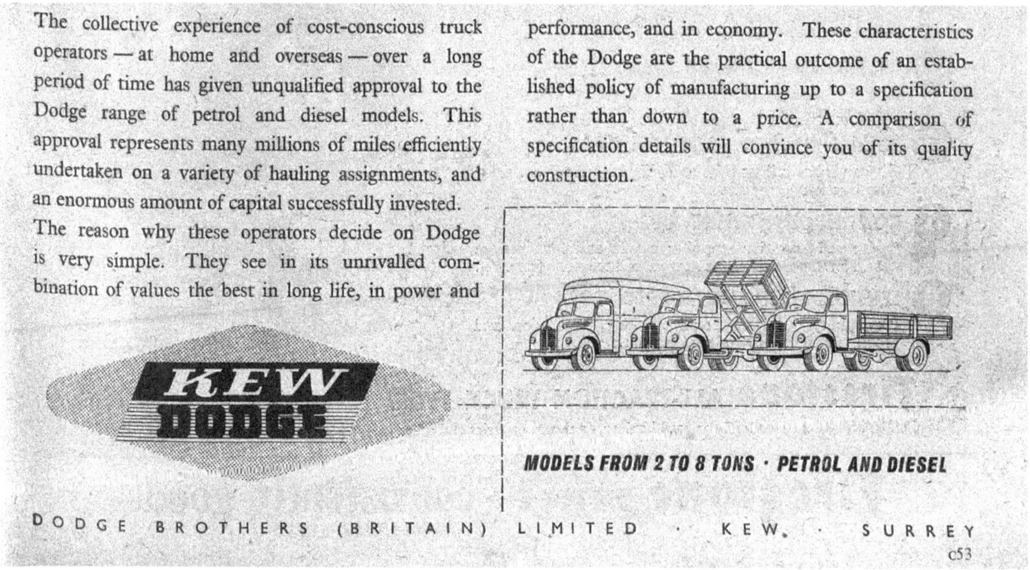

During the Second World War, the factory was turned over to military aircraft production, making parts for the Handley Page Halifax bomber. After the war the production turned to Dodge trucks and lorries, again using the name 'Kew' as a prefix. In 1967 the factory was closed and production moved to Dunstable. The site is now the Kew Retail Park, shown in the image below. (Upper: Graces Guide))

Firestone, Brentford

Without doubt one of London's most famous factories, the Firestone Tyre & Rubber Company's huge building on the Great West Road at Brentford held a strong appeal for many who saw it. Finished in a space of seven months in 1928, 'Firestone's' was another of Wallis Gilbert & Partners' designs. Looking like an art deco palace and mounted on a raised bank above road level, there was no way that the occupants of passing vehicles could not be impressed by the building. The gleaming white façade hid the fact that behind it, workers toiled away making the tyres that would go on many of the vehicles that thundered past outside. A big tradition was the placing of Christmas trees and festive illuminations, and this added to the sense of its community value. In 1978 the company celebrated its fiftieth year of making rubber products and employing so many West London people. However, sadly Firestone closed its doors the following year, due to an economic downturn for the parent company in America. The demolition of this mighty factory took place in 1980, despite desperate attempts to save it by those that loved it. The building that replaced it couldn't contrast more strongly and it is unlikely it will be as fondly remembered when its demolition comes. Fortunately there are some surviving elements – the surrounding fencing, posts, lamps and steps remain and at the Museum of London you can view the front gates and fragments of decorative tiles. (Upper: Lukas Novotny, Lower: Hounslow Borough Archives)

Chocolate & Sweets

Easter Egg production, Nestle, Hayes, 1950s. (Nestlé Historical Archives, Nestlé, Vevey)

Nestlé, Hayes

The site has a rich history. The first factory on the site was opened in 1914 by Eugen Sandow, the World's Strongest Man of 1889, where he produced his 'Health and Strength Cocoa'. The site was bought by Nestlé in 1929, and the factory produced chocolate products. At the outbreak of the Second World War Nestlé had perfected a way of producing instant coffee, and it was from the Hayes site that production went into overdrive, supplying troops fighting overseas. The factory closed in 2015, with all but its impressive art deco office block being demolished for housing. The lower image shows chocolate production in the 1950s. (Nestlé Historical Archives)

Wrigleys, Wembley

William Wrigley set up a British sales division in 1911 but sales were slow until gum-chewing was taken up by troops in the trenches. After the war ended sales increased, and it was decided to start production in a new factory. Eleven acres of former British Empire Exhibition land at Wembley were purchased and a Wallis Gilbert & Partners-designed building was completed in 1927. The site was right next to the London & North Western Railway, and a spur ran off for the factory. By the 1930s the site was producing 300,000 sticks of gum a day. By 1970 the company had outgrown the Wembley factory (pictured below circa 1930) and moved to Plymouth, taking 25 per cent of its workforce with it. The building survives and contains a number of different businesses. (Upper: Graces Guide, Lower: Author's Collection)

An aerial view of the Factory of Maynards Limited at Vale Road, Finsbury Park, London, N.4 occupying a quarter of a million square feet of covered floor space.
ESTABLISHED 1896

Maynards, Harringay

Famous for their wine gums, Maynards started in Stamford Hill, in 1880, with the two Maynard brothers, Charles and Tom, making sweets in their kitchen. They were sold in Charles's wife's shop next door. By 1896 the brothers had formed their own company and with sales increasing, the company moved to a new factory on Vale Road, Harringay, in 1906. The photograph below shows part of the factory and staff in the mid-1920s. (Cadbury Archives (Mondelez Europe))

The photo at the top shows production at Vale Road in the early 1980s. Maynards was bought by Trebor in 1985, and the Harringay facility closed in 1998. The factory buildings remain and are used for various businesses, including the Oriental Carpet Company. It is quite remarkable how much of the factory remains, and it is amongst one of the most complete of its age and type in London. A visit to the site will show you some rather nice decoration, as seen below. (Upper: Cadbury Archive (Mondelez Europe))

Barratts, Wood Green

The company was started by George Osborne Barratt in the 1840s, at No. 32 Shepherdess Walk, Hoxton. His first success was the accidentally formulated 'Stickjaw' toffee. Neighbouring properties were bought and absorbed. By 1880 Barratt needed more room and so bought an old piano factory, at Mayes Road in Wood Green. The factory had been built for Allsopp & Co., and was owned by a Mr Ivory! Ongoing success meant that new buildings were constructed and the site ended up as a large sprawling complex. Barratt's was acquired by Bassett's of Sheffield for almost £4 million in 1966. The Wood Green factory was closed with the loss of 750 jobs in 1975. Fortunately, a great deal of the factory remains and has been repurposed as a business centre.

Clarnico, Hackney Wick
The company started in 1872, in Hackney Wick, as Clarke, Nicholls & Coombs – the brand name was abbreviated to 'Clarnico' – and first made candied peel and jam before moving onto confectionery. The first part of the factory stood on Carpenters Road. By 1890 the company employed 1,500 people, mainly women. Deliveries of sugar arrived on the nearby Lee Navigation. (LB Hackney Archives)

By the interwar period it had 700 confectionery lines, and after the Second World War it had outgrown its original factories and had a huge new one built in Waterden Road. Clarnico was bought by Trebor in 1969 for £900,000. The manufacturing was run down in the early 1970s, but the buildings remained right up until the redevelopment of the area for the 2012 London Olympics. Clarnico's is remembered by two developments: 'Sweetwater' and Clarnico Quay. One confectionery line survives to this day, in the form of Mint Creams, made by the inheritors of the company, CadburysMondelez. (Upper: Author's Collection, Lower: Andy Byrnes)

Trebor, Forest Gate

Formed in 1907 by Messrs Woodcock, King, Robertson and Marks. The factory was built around a row of pre-existing houses called Trebor Terrace, just off Katherine Road, and this was the inspiration for the trade name Trebor, created in 1918. A new modernist-style factory was built on the site in 1935. By the 1950s the company needed more space and took over an old coach factory in Woodford. At the close of the 1960s Trebor claimed to be the largest confectionery maker in the UK and exported to fifty countries across the world. However, the game was up by 1989 when Cadburys bought the company. The old factory is now a residential block. (Cadbury Archives (Mondelez Europe))

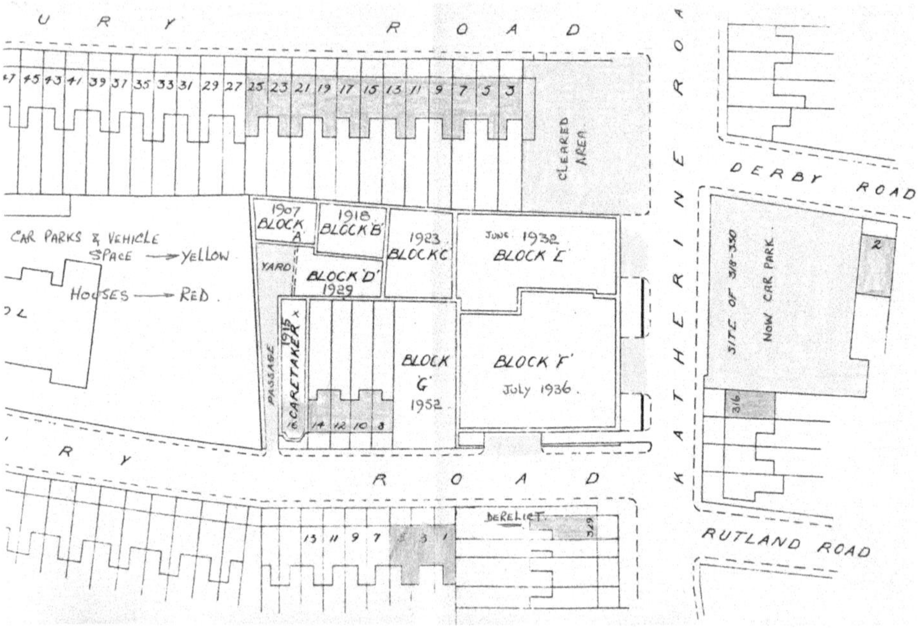

Biscuits

McVities production, Harlesden, 1950s. (Pladis UK)

McVitie (& Price), Harlesden

McVitie & Price was formed in Edinburgh during the 1880s. Like its competitors, it realised it needed to capture the London market. They found a site in what was greenfields on Waxlow Road, Harlesden, conveniently sited between the London & North Western Railway and the Grand Union Canal. A prestigious and stately brick-built factory was opened in 1902. The images on this page show the factory in its final stages of completion. The idyllic countryside surrounding the buildings is a clear contrast with the industrial landscape of today. Sales and expansion continued over the years and by 1936 the factory was employing 2,000 workers, producing thirty different varieties of biscuits. (Pladis Global (UK))

The image above shows a worker preparing the famous digestive biscuits for wrapping. In 1948 McVitie & Price incorporated automated production methods, among the first to do so within the industry. That year also saw the company merge with its Scottish competitor Macfarlane Lang, becoming United Biscuits. During the 1970s the Waxlow Road factory was comprehensively redeveloped, sadly losing a great deal of the old buildings in the process. The image below shows a works plan from 1991. McVitie's still makes biscuits at Harlesden, under the ownership of Pladis, and if you are lucky and the wind is blowing the right way, you can smell the wonderful aroma of Hobnobs being baked! (Pladis Global (UK))

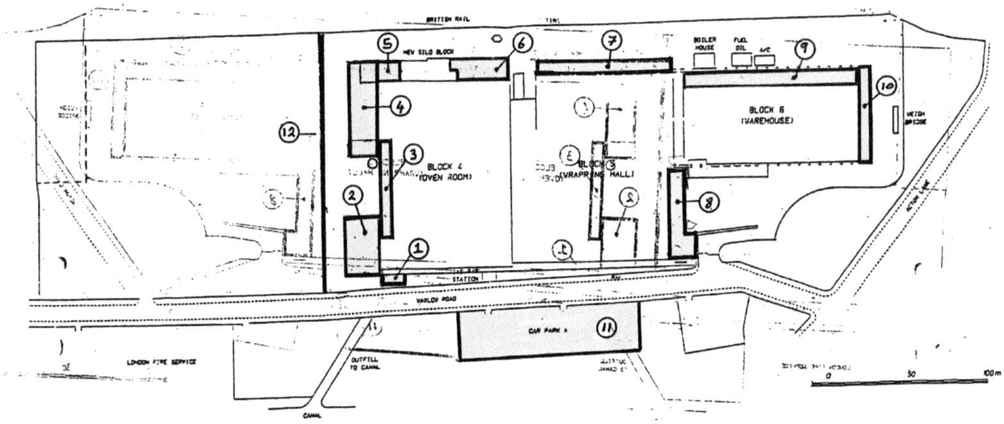

1 SUB STATION
2 ADMINISTRATION AND TECHNICAL BLOCK
3 FAT STORAGE AREA
4 SMALL INGREDIENT HANDLING
5 SERVICES AREA
6 SYRUP AND CHOCOLATE STORAGE
7 PRODUCTION AND ENGINEERING BLOCK
8 AMENITIES BLOCK
9 PACKAGING STORE
10 SERVICES BLOCK
11 CAR PARK
12 NEW SITE BOUNDRAY

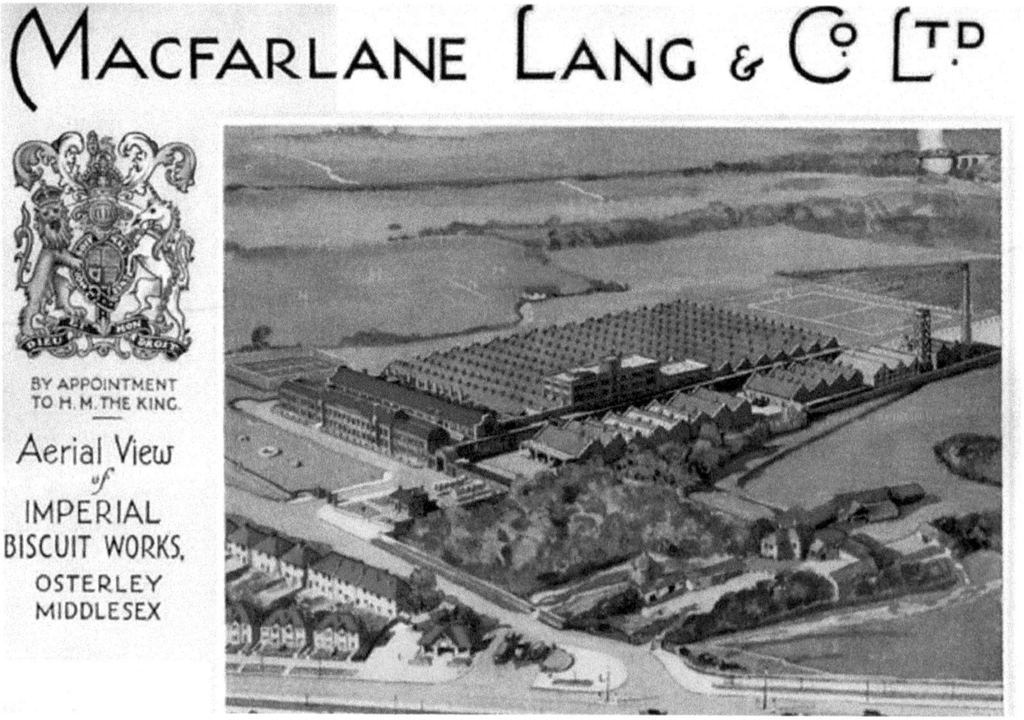

Macfarlane Lang, Osterley

James Lang started his company in Glasgow in 1817, joined by his nephew John Macfarlane. Demand in London meant the establishment of Lang's first factory, the Imperial Biscuit Works, in Fulham in 1903. They moved to a new factory in Osterley in 1929 on what was agricultural land, and the farm was kept (see the image above) to contribute fresh fruit to the factory. Sadly, this was obliterated by the Gillette factory in the mid-1930s. The vast five-acre site employed 2,500 workers. The factory was served well by the new Great West Road, and by a spur from the Great Western Railway. (Upper: Pladis Global (UK), Lower: Hounslow Borough Archives)

In 1948 the company merged with McVitie & Price to become United Biscuits. With the phasing out of the Macfarlane Lang brand during the 1960s, production was turned over to other United Biscuit brands, including Crawfords. The images on this page date from the last few years at the Osterley site before it closed in 1982. The factory was completely demolished and a Tesco superstore now stands on the site, so a biscuit connection survives in a tenuous way. (Pladis Global (UK))

Kemps, Cricklewoood

The company was established in 1904 as George Kemp Ltd at Brewery Road, Islington. By 1930 it had done well enough to have a very large factory built on the North Circular Road, next to the Staples factory. Amongst the large range of products they manufactured, Kemp's seemed to specialise in highly decorative tins of biscuits, and there are many examples to be found for sale as second-hand items to this day. The Midlands-based bakery Scribbans bought out the company in 1946, and the company was renamed Scibbans-Kemp. Wrights Biscuits from north-east England bought Scibbans-Kemp in 1962 and the Cricklewood factory closed in the same year. The factory was eventually demolished and the site is now home to a vast, characterless metal shed occupied by several businesses. (Upper: LCC Municipal, Lower: Author's Collection)

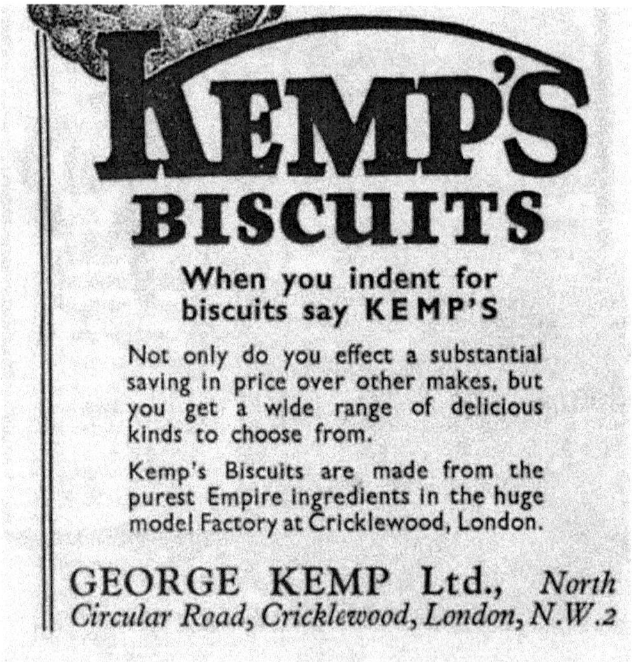

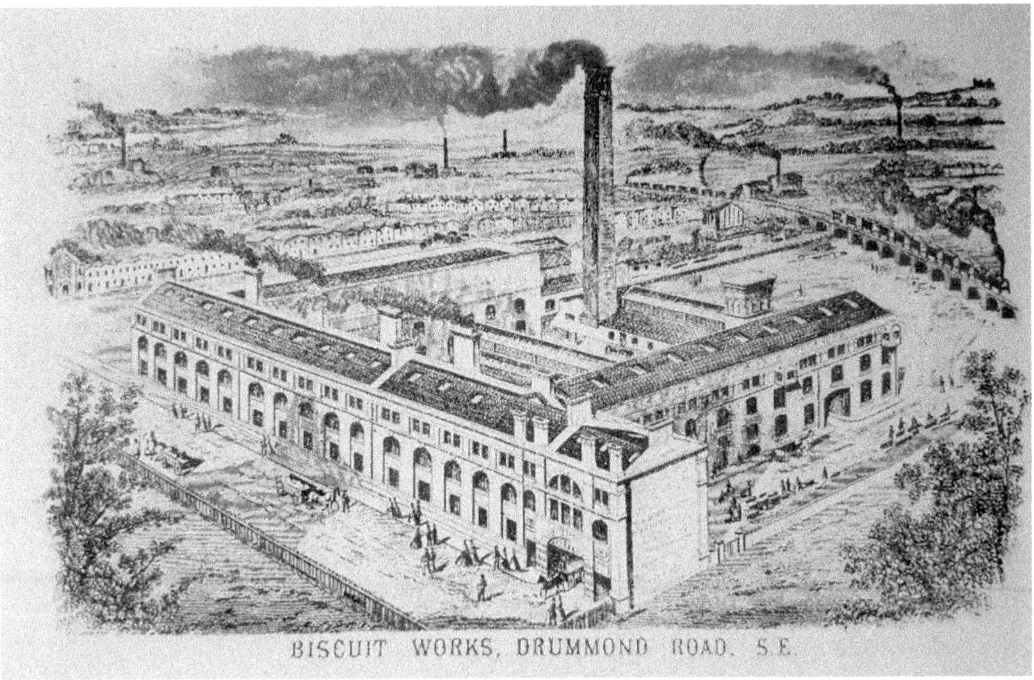

Peek, Freans, Bermondsey
James Peek founded a tea importing business with his brothers in 1821. As time moved on, he looked to diversify the business and hired his niece's husband, George Frean, who was a miller and baker, to start a biscuit-making operation, Peek, Frean & Co. A factory was opened at Dock Head, Bermondsey, in 1857. By 1865 the company was doing so well that it needed larger premises and bought a nearby ten-acre former market garden, off Drummond Road, to build a large new factory. As the illustrations on this page show, the complex grew rapidly. (Peek Frean's Museum)

The Drummond Road factory was so large that it became known as 'Biscuit Town' and employed a large number of local people. Peek, Freans had a strong family approach to its employees, with free on-site medical, dental and optical facilities. It also had an on-site bank, post office and fire station. The image above dates from around 1970, when the factory was upgraded, sadly losing a large number of the original buildings in the process, in particular the impressive clock tower. In 1921 the company joined up with former rivals Huntley & Palmer, followed in 1961 by Jacobs. The resulting conglomerate, Associated Biscuit Makers, was then bought out by Nabisco in 1982. The inevitable restructuring lead to the Drummond Road factory closing in 1989. (Peek Frean's Museum)

Food & Drink

J. Lyons & Co. Bakery receipt, 1949. (eBay)

Lyons & Co., Hammersmith and Greenford
The highly successful mass catering, food and drinks company was founded by the Salmon and Gluckstein family in 1884. Looking for larger production facilities, it eventually purchased a former piano works called Cadby Hall on the Hammersmith Road in 1899. The factory was huge and grew over the years to accommodate a vast range of production, from bread to ice cream. The company once again needed more space and in 1921 it opened a large complex at Greenford, on what was open land. Access to the Great Western Railway was on one side and the Grand Union Canal on the other. Despite its great history, Lyons eventually succumbed to financial problems and was broken up in the late 1970s. Both factories no longer exist. (Upper: Britain from Above, Lower: Author's Collection)

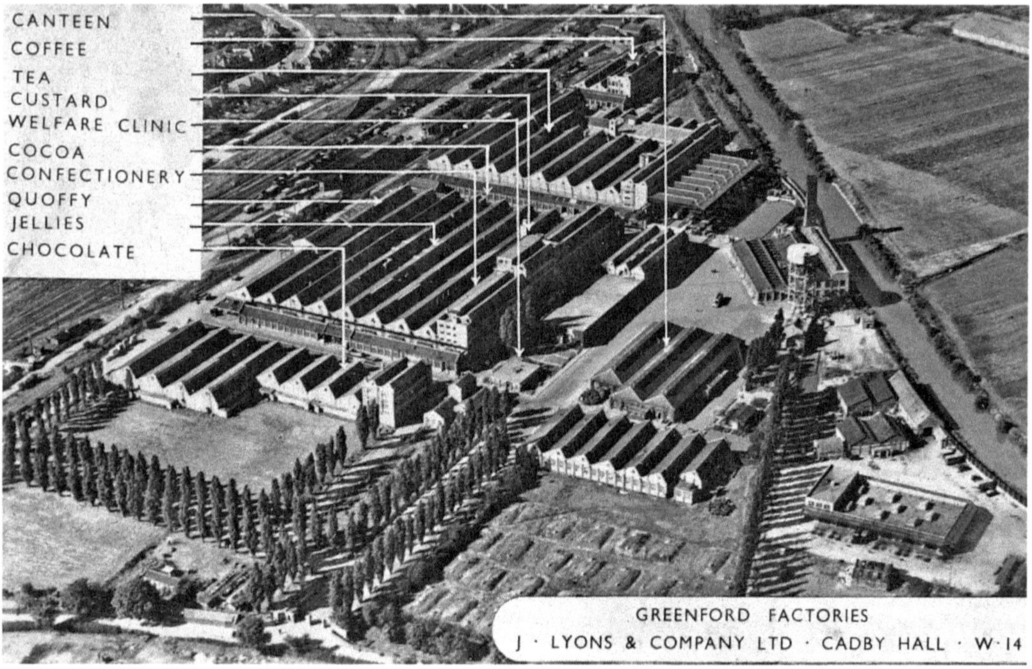

Heinz, Harlesden
H. J. Heinz started its British production at a former pickle factory in Peckham in 1905, but moved to a twenty-acre greenfield site at Waxlow Road, Harlesden. The large factory was opened in 1925, conveniently close to the Grand Union Canal and the Great Western Railway. The building made full use of signage, listing a number of their top-selling items. The image above is the reverse side of a Heinz company envelope mailed in 1938, and shows the canal running beside the building. The factory was bombed twice in the Second World War, but was rebuilt rapidly on both occasions. By the 1950s, the fifty-three-acre site employed over 5,000 people, but after company restructuring, this figure was down to 2,000 by 1980. The company eventually closed the factory in 2000, and sadly nothing remains of this once important local landmark. (Author's Collection)

Above: Sarson's, Bermondsey
Vinegar was made on the site seen above, in Tanner Street, from the 1890s through to 1968.

Left: Hartley's, Bermondsey
William Pickles Hartley, who already operated a factory in Liverpool, opened his jam factory on Green Walk, Bermondsey, in 1902. The handsome building (seen below) employed 2,000 people at its height. Production ceased in around 1960 and moved to Cambridgeshire. In the early 2000s the building was converted into apartments.

Schweppes, West Hendon

The iconic mineral water and soda water bottlers Schweppes had operated in a number of sites in central London since 1792. The company built a new facility in West Hendon in 1896, sited conveniently on an artesian well, and next to the Edgware Road and the Midland Railway. The setting was rather idyllic, with a large set of stables for the horse-drawn delivery vans. A large makeover completed in the early 1960s (see below) included an eye-catching fountain to replicate the company's trademark. The factory closed in 1980, and the site is now a car showrooms and the famous theatrical outfitters Angels. (Upper: London Borough of Barnet, Lower: Francis Frith Collection)

Lucozade, Brentford
Invented by a Newcastle-upon-Tyne chemist in 1927, and originally called 'Glucozade', the brand was bought by Beechams in the 1930s and renamed. Opened on the Great West Road in 1953, the real genius of the factory was the use of an illuminated sign on the side of the building. The design utilised a poured bottle dispensing its sparkling contents into a rather elegant goblet, a sequenced set of light bulbs adding to the illusion. By the time the raised M4 motorway had arrived in 1959, this signage came into its own, and for the next forty years the Lucozade sign was a welcoming sight to those coming into London from the West. Sadly, in 2004 the then redundant factory was demolished but such was the sign's importance, a new placing was made further back up the road. In 2015 the sign was replaced by a digital ad-screen. The site is now an Audi car showrooms. (GlaxoSmithKline)

Smith's Crisps, Brentford

Frank Smith was working in the family greengrocery business, and in 1913 he started making potato crisps, initially from a lock up garage at the rear of the Crown Hotel in Cricklewood. The business became incredibly successful very quickly and by 1925 a new factory and head office was built on the Great West Road, in Brentford. (Hounslow Borough Archives)

The building was adorned with huge advertising designs, which lasted way past the company's departure in 1970, surviving under steel cladding. This wonderful hidden treasure was revealed briefly before everything was demolished for an office complex built for Data General in the mid-1980s. The Smiths brand continues under the ownership of the American-owned Walker's snack company in Leicestershire.

Around the House

Blade wrapping, Gillette, Osterley, 1936. (Hounslow Borough Archives)

Hoover, Perivale

The Ohio-based Hoover Suction Sweeper Company Limited set up a UK sales office in Regent Street in 1919. As sales grew, it became apparent that a new factory should be built to make the company's vacuum cleaners, and a sizeable plot of land was purchased in Perivale beside the new Western Avenue. Opening in 1932, the grand factory and offices were designed by Wallis Gilbert & Partners. The frontage used a new material called 'Snocrete' that achieved a brilliant white finish. Subtle tile decoration in orange, blue and green, and a stunning entrance, all added to a building that truly dazzled the passer-by, and the huge 'By Appointment' royal coat of arms (sadly no longer there) signified that Hoover was the vacuum cleaner to buy. Increased sales success lead to further extensions in 1934 and 1935. In addition, 1938 saw a standalone two-storey canteen block built for the staff. During the Second World War, the factory's highly visible appearance was dulled down, covered with huge camouflage netting, and production was turned over to military aircraft components. (Upper: Lukas Novotny, lower: Graces Guide)

After the war, production of vacuum cleaners resumed and the company continued to invest in the Perivale complex, building a large research and development block at the rear. Sadly, economic changes forced Hoover to close the factory in 1987, after a long winding-down period. For two years the buildings lay empty and forlorn, the royal warrant was removed (they can only be used if the owner is in occupation), and its preservation was secured by a Grade II listing. In 1989 Tesco sympathetically redeveloped the site at the rear as a supermarket, and the restored offices at the front were occupied by Gallaher, the tobacco company. More recently the offices have been redeveloped as apartments.

Smith's, Cricklewood

Samuel Smith started making watches and instruments in Newington Causeway in the 1850s. By the outbreak of the First World War military contracts, aircraft instrumentation in particular, forced Smiths to build a new factory in Cricklewood, by the side of the Edgware Road and, conveniently, right next to Handley Page's factory. By the 1930s Smiths had moved into domestic clock and watch making, as well as instrumentation for motor vehicles. Unfortunately the 1980s saw the Cricklewood factory closed and Smiths Group now operates at a number of locations across the globe. The Cricklewood site is now a retail area. (Smiths Group plc)

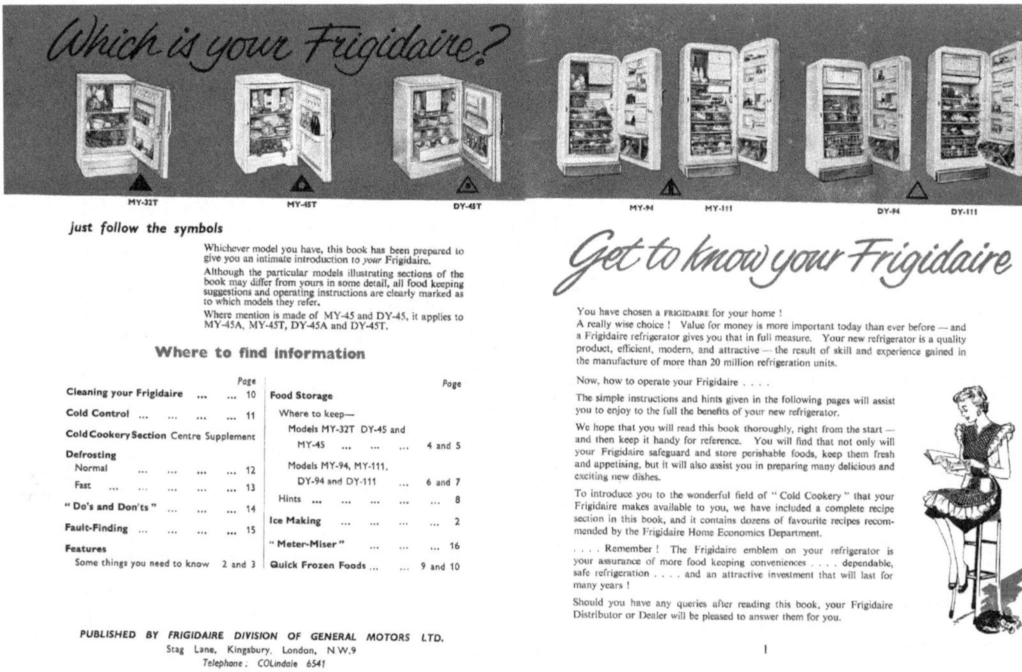

Which is your Frigidaire?

MY-32T MY-45T DY-45T MY-94 MY-111 DY-94 DY-111

just follow the symbols

Whichever model you have, this book has been prepared to give you an intimate introduction to *your* Frigidaire.

Although the particular models illustrating sections of the book may differ from yours in some detail, all food keeping suggestions and operating instructions are clearly marked as to which models they refer.

Where mention is made of MY-45 and DY-45, it applies to MY-45A, MY-45T, DY-45A and DY-45T.

Where to find information

PUBLISHED BY FRIGIDAIRE DIVISION OF GENERAL MOTORS LTD.
Stag Lane, Kingsbury, London, N.W.9
Telephone: COLindale 6541

Get to know your Frigidaire

You have chosen a FRIGIDAIRE for your home !

A really wise choice ! Value for money is more important today than ever before — and a Frigidaire refrigerator gives you that in full measure. Your new refrigerator is a quality product, efficient, modern, and attractive — the result of skill and experience gained in the manufacture of more than 20 million refrigeration units.

Now, how to operate your Frigidaire . . . .

The simple instructions and hints given in the following pages will assist you to enjoy to the full the benefits of your new refrigerator.

We hope that you will read this book thoroughly, right from the start — and then keep it handy for reference. You will find that not only will your Frigidaire safeguard and store perishable foods, keep them fresh and appetising, but it will also assist you in preparing many delicious and exciting new dishes.

To introduce you to the wonderful field of " Cold Cookery " that your Frigidaire makes available to you, we have included a complete recipe section in this book, and it contains dozens of favourite recipes recommended by the Frigidaire Home Economics Department.

. . . . Remember ! The Frigidaire emblem on your refrigerator is your assurance of more food keeping conveniences . . . . dependable, safe refrigeration . . . . and an attractive investment that will last for many years !

Should you have any queries after reading this book, your Frigidaire Distributor or Dealer will be pleased to answer them for you.

1

Frigidaire, Kingsbury

When General Motors moved its vehicle manufacturing to Luton in the late 1920s, it immediately converted the old Airco main assembly plant to the manufacture of refrigerators and industrial air conditioning equipment. The plant's main entrance moved to Stag Lane (where the formal gardens are in the photo below). The company expanded operations as the years passed, but the change of ownership to Electrolux in 1979 saw the factory close, with the loss of many jobs. The Edgware Road site was redeveloped as an Asda superstore, and the rear as a trading estate, in the 1980s. (Upper: Author's Collection, Lower: Britain from Above)

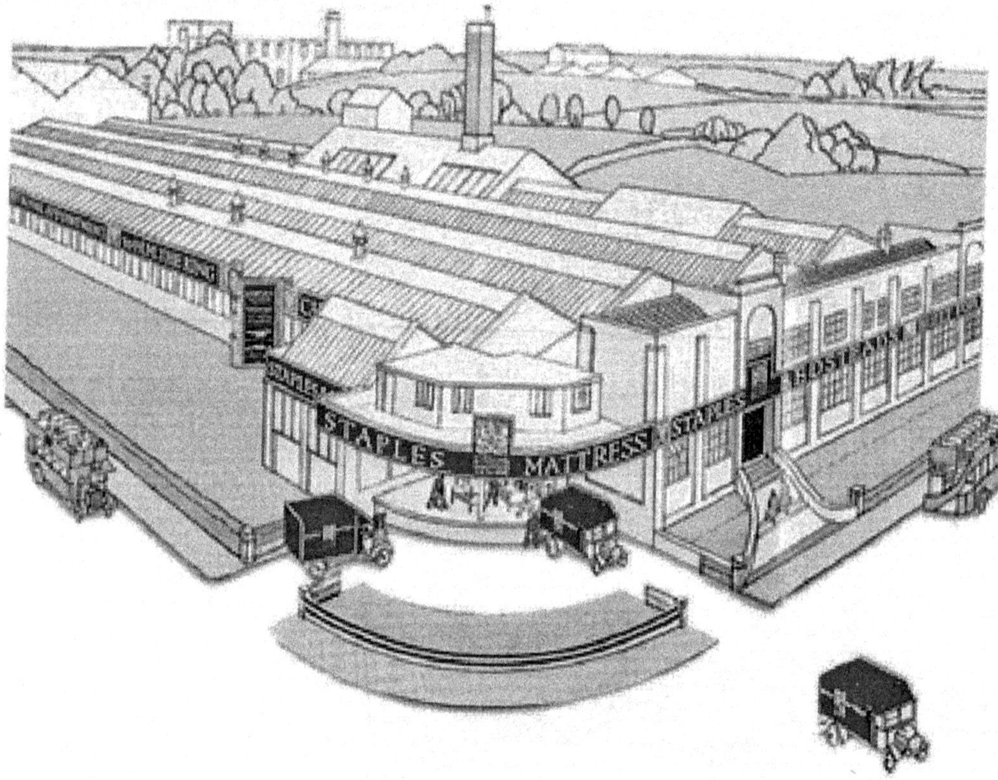

Staples, Cricklewood

The makers of fine mattresses by appointment to the royal family was set up by Ambrose Heal in the Edwardian era. By 1925 the company required a new factory and found a site on the corner of the Edgware Road and the new North Circular. At this time the area was almost open countryside, and Staples's nearest neighbour was Bentley Motors. The factory building was adorned with attractive and distinctive signage, and very quickly this part of Cricklewood became known as 'Staples Corner'. The company had left by the early 1970s, and the site was redeveloped. In the 1990s another Staples occupied the new buildings: the American office supplies company of the same name. More recently, the corner has seen the erection of a new Jaguar car showroom. (Upper: Author's Collection, Left: Graces Guide)

Macleans, Brentford

Alexander Maclean started his pharmaceutical and toiletries company in Paddington in 1919. By 1932 the company had built a new factory on the corner of Boston Manor Road and the Great West Road. The elaborate frontage featured gardens and an illuminated art deco glass fountain, presumably to convey freshness and health. The image above shows the factory decorated for the 1937 Coronation. Best known for its toothpaste and stomach powders, Macleans was bought by Beechams in 1938. Production carried on until the late 1960s, but by 1969 the factory had been bought by Rank Audio Visual. The site was cleared in the 1990s for the company who own the Macleans brand, GlaxoSmithKline, to build a huge new HQ on the site (shown below). (Upper: GlaxoSmithKline)

Beecham, Brentford
Beechams was once a mighty pharmaceuticals and household products company and had a number of factories on the Great West Road in Brentford. In the late 1950s it moved into the splendid building above, which was originally built for Simmonds Aerocessories in 1937. By the late 1980s Beechams had merged with the US company SmithKine, and in the late 1990s production had moved to other factories outside London. (GlaxoSmithKline)

Glaxo, Greenford
The company had started as Joseph Nathan & Co. in 1873, producing a baby milk formula called 'Glaxo'. Over the years the company grew as a major pharmaceuticals company, and in 1935 opened its new laboratories on Greenford Road. The company is now part of the large GlaxoSmithKline company. The Greenford buildings were vacated in the late 1990s, and the main building repurposed as offices.

Gillette, Isleworth

The American razor and shaving products company opened its landmark factory on the corner of the Great West Road and Syon Lane in 1936. The huge clock tower (which housed a water tank) was supposedly meant to resemble an upturned razor. Together with the Firestone factory (which was very close by), this building was the height of interwar showpiece factories and has become a much-loved landmark. The last of the area's big manufacturers, Gillette ceased production in 2006 and moved out a year later. The site is currently being used as a storage facility and is Grade II listed. (Upper: Hounslow Borough Archives)

Ever-Ready, Walthamstow

With its origins in America, the British Ever Ready Electric Company, or BEREC, was formed in 1906, manufacturing electric lamps, torches and dry cell batteries. The company had a number of different factories in both the Midlands and London, and in around 1930 it took over and redeveloped the old AEC bus and lorry works on Forest Road, Walthamstow. Covering a floor area of 175,000 square feet, the factory produced radio high tension batteries and dry cells for electric torches. At its height the factory employed 2,000 people. Production ceased in the 1970s, and the site has more recently been a trading estate. (Graces Guide)

The new Walthamstow factory of the Ever Ready Co. (Great Britain), Ltd.

A FLEET OF BRITISH CARS IN USE BY THE ROYAL SOVEREIGN PENCIL CO. LTD.

Royal Sovereign Pencils, Neasden

Formed in the early 1920s by the marriage of two old companies, Arthur Johnson and E. Wolff & Son, the company was based in a collection of factory buildings off Neasden Lane. Supply to Government departments during the Second World War was sufficient to not bother with any other customers. I was unable to pin down when the factory closed but the company had been bought up by the German company of Staedtler by the late 1980s. The Neasden site is now a trading estate (see below). (Upper: Graces Guide)

Winsor & Newton, Harrow
Famous for its artists' supplies, the company arrived in 1937 and left in 2011. (Colart)

Kodak, Harrow
The Eastman company had a brand new factory built in 1891 on what was then Middlesex countryside. The site was right next to the London & North Western Railway. The company was a major employer and contributor to the economy of the local area. Sadly, changes in the photographic industry and restructuring resulted in the eventual closure of the complex in 2016, ending a 125-year history. The site is currently being redeveloped as large housing development called Eastman Village. The landmark white chimney will be preserved.

Dubreq (Stylophone), Cricklewood

The world's first hand-held pocket electronic organ was invented by Brian Jarvis, co-owner of the Dubreq recording studios, in 1967. Production started the year after and early exposure on television created enormous demand. The image below shows the compact factory that was based on Cricklewood Lane. Its big claim to fame was that it was used by David Bowie in his 1969 hit 'Space Oddity'. Thousands of these incredible devices were made, and they became a big hit with all ages. Production ended in 1975, presumably as interest waned and there were better developments by other manufacturers. The device was resurrected in 2007 by Ben Jarvis, son of the device's inventor, and has developed into a range of types, designed at the Hastings offices. (Dubreq)

Park Royal

London's industries were scattered across the capital in a haphazard way, in a lot of cases growing like weeds do: in gaps between other developments. Some companies decided that they would remove themselves totally from the congestion of the inner area and move out to what was green fields, good examples of this being Kodak in Harrow and McVities in Harlesden in the late Victorian years. The coming of the new arterial roads in the 1920s allowed expansion out into the open countryside. One area of what had been open land ended up being one of London's major industrial zones. Park Royal in West London is an extensive industrial and commercial estate in the far north of Acton, between the Western Avenue and the Grand Union Canal, covering the boroughs of Brent and Ealing.

The area was once Twyford – which means 'Two Fords'. The coming of the Grand Union Canal in 1801, and the railways in 1866 at Willesden Junction, was the start of the area's development. Things really started in 1900 when the Royal Agricultural Society bought a large piece of land from the Twyford Abbey Estate, to create a permanent showground. Twyford Abbey was never really an 'abbey'; it had been a manor house that was remodelled to look like a gothic building by its new owner in 1806. The German Roman Catholic Alexian Brotherhood used the abbey as a rest home between 1902 and 1988. The Royal Agricultural Society was set up in 1838, and held shows throughout the country displaying the latest achievements in agriculture, including farm machinery and animals. The 1879 show was held in Willesden on land that became Queens Park. That show went badly due to inclement weather. As a result of this, it was decided that costs would be reduced if they chose a permanent venue – which is where Twyford comes in.

The Royal Agricultural society spent £70,000 on the site, and it was opened in 1903 by the Prince of Wales and was named Park Royal in his honour. Names of roads show the connection – Coronation Road and Victoria Road in particular. The shows, however, were not a success and the Society abandoned the site, deciding instead on touring the show around UK. One of the first big manufactures in the area was McVitie & Price, which opened its huge factory in Waxlow Road in 1903; the company claimed it was the largest biscuit factory in the world. The factory sat on land between the Great Western Railway and the Grand Union Canal, making it perfect for transportation.

In the First World War former showgrounds, which had lain idle, were turned over to the war effort. There were two large munitions factories, referred to as the National Filling Factories, plus a National Box Factory, an Army clothing store. There was also a large compound for horses of the Royal Army Service Corps, and a prisoner of war camp. At the end of the First World War, the Government sold off its interests in the land to Allnatt Properties, which became the major landlord.

During the 1920s two new major arterial roads, the North Circular and Western Avenue, were constructed, skirting the outside of the Park Royal area, making it very attractive to industry. This, on top of what was cheap land, led to rapid industrial growth. At the height of its development in the 1930s, the landlords oversaw the building of two factories a week. By 1932 there were eighty-three factories on the site, employing over 13,000 people.

H. J. Heinz built its factory in 1925. By 1934 the company was bringing on by rail eight railway wagons of Welsh coal to use for its steam plant to sterilise food containers. The company was a huge employer, hitting a peak of 3,500 staff in 1964. Guinness arrived in the mid-1930s, building the world's largest brewery, designed by Sir Giles Gilbert Scott. Other Park Royal manufacturers included Rizla, the cigarette paper makers, based near the Stonebridge Park area; Cheesbrough Ponds, who made Vaseline; Elizabeth Arden, the cosmetics company, in North Acton; Cerebos, the salt company; Wall's, maker of sausages and ice cream on two different sites, Friary Road and Atlas Road; Park Royal Vehicles (who built the Routemaster bus bodies); Mulliner Park Ward (later Rolls-Royce), the coachbuilders; and Waterlows Printers, who were a major worldwide engraver of currency, postage stamps, stocks and bond certificates, as well as the printers of the *Radio Times* and *Listener* magazines. The Second World War saw the area hit badly by air raids. Things returned to normal after the war and new factories were built, but by the time of the UK's economic downturn in the 1970s, Park Royal was hit hard, with many manufacturers either closing or moving out, hastened in particular by the roads, which were too narrow for big vehicles.

Park Royal at the time of writing is still a manufacturing area, although its predominant output is ready meals and pre-made sandwiches. But the greater bulk of its former factory areas are now given over to warehousing of goods made in other parts of the world. The area is also seeing the ingress of housing, in particular on the former Guinness Brewery site, with the erection of huge luxury apartment blocks.

Facts and Anecdotes

In the course of my research for this book, I found some rather interesting facts and anecdotes. For example, I was contacted by Bruce Hanson, whose father worked at the Bentley Motors Cricklewood factory and recalled that when the race cars returned from the Le Mans 24-hour race there was still orange peel on the floor of the car. It had been left by the drivers, who clearly ate them to keep up their energy levels. His father's first job at the factory was to stamp loads of tiny Bentley emblems over the entire engine sump cover (a part of the car an owner would rarely see). He also remembered that the foreman's final test was to balance a penny on the valve cover of a running engine; if it fell over the engine had to be stripped down and rebuilt.

Lesney Products, the manufacturers of Matchbox toys, owned a fleet of old buses, painted in their company colours (why waste a good marketing opportunity?), to pick up their workers. Staff would wait at designated stops en route.

Guinness owned a herd of milk cows, which they inherited from the nearby farm of Twyford Abbey. The milk was used in the company's canteens.

Britains made shrapnel to go inside munitions during the First World War, using the lead alloy that it would have normally used in its toy soldiers. When the war was over the company bought back the unused metal at considerably less than its market value, allowing it an early and profitable return to toy production. The company was a pioneer of home workers. The practice started when a woman who became pregnant asked if she could do product finishing at home. Britain's liked the idea and ended up employing 3,000 home workers. It established six depots around North and East London to distribute and pick up the production.

Firestone started a Christmas tradition by having festive trees and illuminated displays in the grounds of its Brentford factory. Photographs of the demolition of the factory in August 1980 clearly show the previous year's trees, complete with illuminations attached, left behind, the company having left early in the year.

There is a tiny trace of Smith's Crisps left in the subway that exists near its old site on the Great West Road. On an access door there is a sign that reads 'Smiths Factory Pumping Station'.

J. Lyon's would hold a special Christmas pudding-making event every year during the 1950s and 1960s, in which the Australian Fruit Marketing Board would donate dried fruit to go into the mix. Celebrities of the day were invited to join in and the whole event would be filmed by British Movietone News. The duo for 1960 was the comedian Charlie Drake and Cliff Richard.

In 1977 Elvis Costello wrote a song called 'The Hoover Factory', and performed it on his demo tape for Stiff Records. The song was an evocation of the palatial building's fading glory. Costello had passed the building on his way to his day job as a data entry clerk at

Elizabeth Arden's cosmetic factory in North Acton, which just happened to be designed by the same architects who designed the Hoover building – Wallis Gilbert & Partners.

There is a great little Peek, Freans museum run by dedicated volunteers, one of them an ex-employee, within the old buildings that remain at the Drummond Road site in Bermondsey. Definitely work a visit, but it is by appointment: visit www.peekfreansmuseum.co.uk.

Working Lives

Factories are nothing without the people who work in them, those who carry out the processes that result in finished goods leaving the building. There was a time, not that long ago, when very large numbers of London's working population were employed in the hundreds of factories spread across its mass. Factory work was almost a rite of passage for many school-leavers. It's a far cry from the present day, when a great many young people will stay on for sixth form, leaving state education at eighteen and then perhaps taking up higher education. Those that don't take this option may go into office-based work. In the past those young people who went into industry may have started in lowly positions, working their way up into more skilled jobs, and it was not unusual for people to stay working at the same company for the rest of their working life.

Employment in the factories was, in the main, monotonous, with long hours and low pay. Compare this with the hopes that people have for employment in the current day. The conditions and pay were offset by the security of a 'steady job', often working for companies that treated their workforce like a family, laying on sports and social activities. A great many of the bigger companies owned their own sports grounds, either close to the factory or further out in healthier areas.

It may seem hard for us in these more selfish and cynical times to understand, but in the past there were many workers who felt proud to work for the companies that employed them, and others who would be desperate to work for them. It wasn't uncommon for some factories to have what was referred to as 'closed shops', where jobs were kept for friends and families. Again, our modern sensibilities would suggest that the companies who owned the factories were happy to do all of these things to keep their workers happy, and that the apparent signs of security and well-being were covering over low wages and exploitation. The simple truth could be that in the past much of the population had lower expectations and that it was sufficient to have a job which paid money to pay the rent and put food on the table.

It's worth considering that a working day in a factory could have meant very different hours of work, with either very early starts, late finishes, or shift work. A great many factories with high demands on their output might operate around the clock. Getting to and from work could be very different too. For some it may have required a walk or a cycle, as car ownership was usually the reserve of the more highly paid worker.

We live in what is referred to as a post-industrial society, and for a great many, the working life of a factory worker is now something that has become history, but we should never forget that our path to a predominately, clean, office-based city was assisted by all those legions of factory workers.

The Ones That Got Away

As I mentioned in the introduction, it was going to be impossible within the format of this book to include every factory, and it meant that I missed out some very notable examples, so in this section I will briefly cover some of these. Please do supplement your interest with internet searches.

Now, I mentioned cars, but I wasn't able to include lorries, trucks and buses, and there was one very important London manufacturer of these vehicles. The Associated Equipment Company or, as it was more commonly known, AEC, started off in Walthamstow in around 1908 and moved to Southall in 1927. AEC was primarily known as the maker of London's buses, the first being the B-Type in 1909, and the last the famous Routemaster, which finished production in 1968. The company also made lorries, which had a reputation for being rough and tough workhorses. Towards the end of its time AEC was owned by the giant British Leyland, and it was in 1980 that that last vehicle rolled off the line and the factory closed.

Another familiar name that didn't make it in was that of EMI, who had a huge complex of factories in Hayes, in West London. The company started off in central London in 1898 as the Gramophone Company, manufacturing what we know as record players, but which were then known as gramophones. In 1907 the company moved out to what was then the Middlesex countryside, on Blythe Road, next to the Great Western Railway. By the following year the company was making records, under the brand name of 'His Master's Voice'. The company made munitions and aircraft parts in both world wars. In 1920 a merger with the UK division of Columbia Records saw a new name for the company, Electrical & Musical Industries (EMI). The Hayes factory was home to early work on television, with the creation of the Marconi-EMI system, which beat the Baird version to become the accepted standard. A great deal of work was done on ground-breaking electronics through until the 1970s, but by the 1980s and 1990s, it was really only records that were being made at the Hayes factory. EMI finally succumbed as a name in 2011. However, a new business kept a small part of the factory site going as 'The Vinyl Factory', pressing records for limited runs for various concerns. A number of the large buildings have been repurposed and are clearly visible from the GWR railway line.

London has long been associated with furniture-making, particularly within small workshops in the East End. One company that escaped the congestion of this part of London was that of Harris Lebus, who built what was to become the world's largest furniture factory in Tottenham Hale, next to the River Lea, in 1900. An enormous variety of wooden furniture was built at the factory; the economies of scale led to the cost of finished products coming down, and Harris Lebus cornered the domestic market. During the First World War the company was turned over to war production and made the wings and fuselages of Handley Page o/100 bombers under contract. In the Second World War the company received the Government contract to make Utility furniture, which was basic and affordable. The post-war period saw new investment into the factory complex, but by the late 1960s Harris Lebus faced competition from cheaper furniture made in Europe. The factory closed in 1969, and housing now covers the site.

Finally, Wall's, makers of sausages and ice cream. The Walls family had been in the butchery trade since the early 1800s in Jermyn Street, gaining a royal warrant in 1812. The first factory opened in Battersea in 1903, followed by a much larger one on the former site of Friary House in Acton in 1920. The company was acquired by Lever Brothers (later to become Unilever) in 1922 and in the same year Walls moved into ice cream production, as a way of using refrigeration equipment in the quieter summer months. In 1956 the company opened a separate meat products plant in Atlas Road, Park Royal. At its peak in 1969 Wall's employed a total of 4,000 people. Over the years Unilever restructured the Wall's operations and the Atlas Road factory closed in around 1978, and the Acton plant in 1988.

The Great West Road

I couldn't do a book about London's industrial past and not include the Great West Road and the industries that lined its route from Chiswick to Osterley, otherwise known as 'The Golden Mile'.

The main routes coming out of London in Victorian times had become congested with the increase in traffic, and the Bath Road leading out westwards was no exception. As it passed through the Brentford High Street section it got particularly bad. Plans had been drawn up to create a relief road as far back as 1837, and a definitive act had been drawn up by the Government in 1914 to build it. The First World War delayed matters, but by 1920 work had started, and on 30 May 1925 the 'Great West Road', running 8½ miles from Chiswick to East Bedfont, was opened by King George V.

For most of its course the new road ran through what had been open countryside and farmland, and this wonder of the motorised age was a great temptation to industry. This was an opportunity for existing and new manufacturers to set up showpiece factories with nothing to get in their way, and local councils were more than happy to give them planning permission, as it was seen as a great opportunity to provide employment at a time when there was a great need for jobs.

The first company to set up on the road was the Hudson Essex Motor Works in 1926; however, within a very short space of time new factories had sprung up, the owners very keen to be part of the industrial showcase the road became. The type of companies who arrived were very much of a type, with most being American and associated with the new consumer market they served. During the course of the book, I have covered a number of the factories, but this section allows me to mention some that didn't make it in.

On the corner of South Ealing Road stood the premises of Alfa-Laval, the British arm of the Swedish company that made milking machinery and oil separators. The company was there from the early 1930s right through to the 1980s. Further on, near the junction of Boston Manor Road, stood the factory of Jantzen, an American company that specialised in knitted swimming costumes. Finished in 1931 to a design that replicated the company's US headquarters, the frontage included an illuminated sign of a woman diving – just one of the many signs that people using the Great West Road had fond memories of. The factory was demolished in the early 1960s to be replaced by an office block now called Great West House.

As we approach the point at which the Grand Union Canal flows under the road, back in 1928, there was built the factory of Trico-Folberth, another American company, famous for making windscreen wipers. Although the building was fairly nondescript in terms of its design, it did possess a particularly interesting neon-lit sign: a fan-shaped globe was tracked across by a wiper-blade. The factory had a notable twenty-one-week strike by female workers in 1976. The company left Brentford in the early 1990s, moving to Wales.

Further along, near where the Great Western Railway once crossed the road, stands what is currently the offices of J. C. Decaux, a wonderful art deco building with a long frontage, built in 1936 for the high street retailer Curry's. This was not a factory as such, but a warehousing operation, with servicing for radios and bicycles. Past this stands what at the time of writing is a vacant building, but which had been opened in 1930 as the factory and offices of Pyrene, the American manufacturer of fire extinguishers and motor accessories. Opening just two years after the Firestone factory that stood opposite, this building is another wonderful art deco concoction designed by Wallis Gilbert & Partners, with a 110-foot-tall central tower. When the company left in the late 1970s it was taken over by the construction company Tarmac. Moving along, on the same side of the road stands what is currently the Syon Clinic, which was built as the factory for Coty cosmetics in 1932. This is probably one of my favourite factory buildings on the Great West Road that is still standing, with a wonderful deco entrance. At its peak the factory employed 400 people making soaps, lipsticks, scents and creams.

Travelling along the 'Golden Mile' section of the Great West Road today, it is perhaps difficult to experience what users of this mighty road felt in the 1930s. For some it was a vulgar show of glitzy, jazz-age architecture, festooned with garish signage and lighting. For others it was an exciting voyage through the wonders of the modern age. It was here that the products of the emerging age of consumerism were made, and perhaps for some of us that age has lead us to the troubled times we live in. For me, I would love to have seen it at its height, because it had literally emerged from the Middlesex fields with such speed, and it conveyed the feeling of a time of optimism and hope that was then crushed by the Second World War. After the war, things were never the same and the frivolous inter-war period seemed a lifetime away, never really to return with the same spirit.

Architecture

One aspect of studying London's industrial past is the buildings themselves. There is such a rich array of architectural styles and types, spanning many decades. We are very fortunate that so many good examples have been saved from demolition, and have been re-purposed, to serve another stage of usage.

Factory owners had different approaches as to how they wanted their buildings to look. For a great many, the buildings were there to serve a purpose and little effort was made to make them look anything other than what they were, and it is those basic structures that have often been demolished without a care. Other manufacturers saw the opportunity to impress, with bold, confident factory buildings that proclaimed to London, and the world, that they were here and they meant business! The examples of these buildings are the ones that create the most passion in people. They have become part of the urban and suburban landscape, and it is now almost unthinkable that we could witness their demise.

No appraisal of London factory architecture could be made without looking at the Great West Road, or in particular what was referred to as 'The Golden Mile', travelling from the Chiswick Roundabout through to Gillette Corner at Osterley. The completion of the new arterial road in 1925 created an opportunity for new factories to be built, and between the late 1920s and the start of the Second World War, they sprung up and lined the road on both sides. This was the start of the 'modern age' and these bold, dramatic and glorious 'palaces of industry' were, in effect, permanent advertisements for the manufacturers who commissioned them. Motoring was very much a pastime of the middle to upper classes at the time, and with the use of attention-grabbing architecture and illuminated signage, go-ahead companies had a constant flow of impressionable customers to exploit.

Without doubt, the 'jewel in the crown' was the Firestone Tyre & Rubber factory, opened in 1928 and built on twenty-six acres in an incredible seven months. Designed by the architectural practice of Wallis, Gilbert & Partners, who were prolific in the inter-war period, no expense was spared in its frontage. This was truly showing-off on a grand scale, unashamedly so, and not surprising when its owners were an American company making a statement. The message was effectively: 'We have arrived and you will buy our tyres!' Not only was it built on a raised pediment but it was finished in a glowing white render, with Egyptian references (fashionable as a result of Howard Carter's discovery of Tutankhamen's tomb in 1922), a huge illuminated clock and a red, neon-lit 'Firestone' sign at the top. But this was nothing more than a grand frontage to impress the motorists, and as you moved around the sides and back of the huge factory things became a little more basic. After all, these were buildings to house manufacturing, and the interiors were the total opposite of the frontages.

This formula of showpiece factories was relatively short-lived. So many of the buildings of this nature that went up were American-owned, and their owners were trying hard to impress themselves on to a new, pliable British consumer class. The post-Second World War period saw a different approach, with less flamboyant architecture in a more stripped-down modernist style.

Notes on the Book

One thought that kept challenging me throughout the making of this book was, 'Will people like it?' I suppose this is not an uncommon concern for authors, and it is heightened by the fact that this is my first published book.

When you decide on the title *London's Industrial Past*, you set yourself up for a fall. I say this because each person reading it has their own take on the subject. So this section allows me to explain myself, I hope.

As I stated in the introduction, the desire to produce this book came from a want to illustrate my interest in the subject matter. I had been describing aspects of London's manufacturing heritage on radio slots, but it was frustrating not to be able to show people what the factories looked like. Being given the opportunity to publish a book gave me that ability, in a small way.

I decided that I would choose manufacturers which, in the main, the reader would be familiar with and brands that still exist and that can still be purchased. I wanted to find areas that people could connect with, that were familiar and perhaps nostalgic. Furthermore, the scope of the contents are very much items that were made for public consumption, with the exception of aircraft! The next aspect to consider was the time period, and to a greater extent the industries I have chosen are those from the twentieth century. I did this because I felt that many readers would be able to relate to a time that was closer to living memory.

With regard to the choice of images, this was very much down to practicalities. It was up to me to locate and pay for the photographs and illustrations used. It became an immense task, and the pressure to get the most relevant and visually interesting images proved to be great. I am a bit of a perfectionist, and I really took the attitude that this would be a book that I would want to buy, and that would hold my attention. I was very fortunate that a number of the images in the book were very kindly supplied without a fee, and I am extraordinarily grateful to the companies and individuals who assisted.

Finding the Industrial Past

There was a time when, for many, the sight of a factory was a less than happy experience. They dotted the landscape of London, and in certain areas they were seemingly everywhere. Much like any other man-made structure, factories became part of the landscape. However, in the latter part of the twentieth century industry went into decline all over the United Kingdom. One by one the companies that had been in London for so long moved out to other, less congested areas. For some it would mean a move to the Home Counties, but in others it could mean a move to much further afield. Sadly, this decline of industry was also a result of closures, and with that it could also mean that the factory buildings would often go too, and in many cases all evidence was wiped away or built over. The most common replacement in the 1970s and 1980s was supermarkets, malls, offices or car parks. In more recent times the common occurrence is the apartment building.

London has been lucky in some cases, with the more impressive, decorative factory buildings kept and reused for different purposes, whether for commerce or accommodation. Notable examples include the wonderful Carreras 'Black Cat' cigarette factory in Mornington Crescent, the Hoover Building in Perivale, and the Trebor factory in Upton Park. But for every survivor there have been losses, most famously the Firestone factory on the Great West Road.

The physical loss of London's industrial structures means that the desire to record evidence of their existence becomes that much more important. As the generations who can remember the industries pass away, it can sometimes seem that history could be lost, and that is why it's important to do things like write books, like this – to act as a reminder that London once made things, lots of things.

How does one go about finding the industrial past? To be sure, in our current times we have the great benefit of the internet to search through seemingly limitless images and texts. Two of my constant online sources are the mind-blowingly excellent Britain from Above.com, and GracesGuide.com. Britain from Above allows the user to search through thousands of aerial photographs of the British Isles, taken from the 1920s through to the 1950s by the Aerofilms company, and it has helped me locate many factories, and even discover ones that I didn't know existed. Grace's Guide is a leading source of historical information on industry and manufacturing in Britain, and contains thousands of pages of information and images on early companies, their products and the people who designed and built them. It has proved an invaluable research aid to me in recent years, and I would like to thank the founders of it.

But no matter how easy and useful the internet is, one should not forget more traditional forms of research – not everything is on the web! I have always used books to do my research, and it was a series of books produced in the 1980s that really inspired my love of industrial history. The books, written by Gavin Weightman, accompanied a series of television programmes called *The Making of Modern London*, produced by the now defunct

London Weekend Television. There were four series in total, and the books that went with each one were superbly written and illustrated.

The other source of information and images is local authority archives. These incredible resources are staffed by hard-working, passionate people who really do have a love for and knowledge of local history. A great many of the images in this book were purchased from the archives of London boroughs, and they provide much-needed income. So I would most definitely recommend a visit; after all, you probably pay for them out of your council tax!

One source of information that is invaluable is collective memory. We are fortunate that we don't have to ask around too far to find people who worked in, or otherwise have memories of, London's industries. For some of these individuals it can be surprising that anyone would be so fascinated by their working lives. If you feel so moved, make a record of their experiences; better still, record them on video or audio. I would also suggest that taking photographs of old factories and their products is also a good idea. Your efforts will be preserving a lost past, and who knows? One day they may end up in a book like this!